Horse
Coloring Book

Get FREE printable coloring pages and discounted book prices sent straight to your e-mail inbox every week!

Sign up at:

www.adultcoloringworld.net

ISBN-13: 978-1533428462
ISBN-10: 1533428468

PREVIEWS:

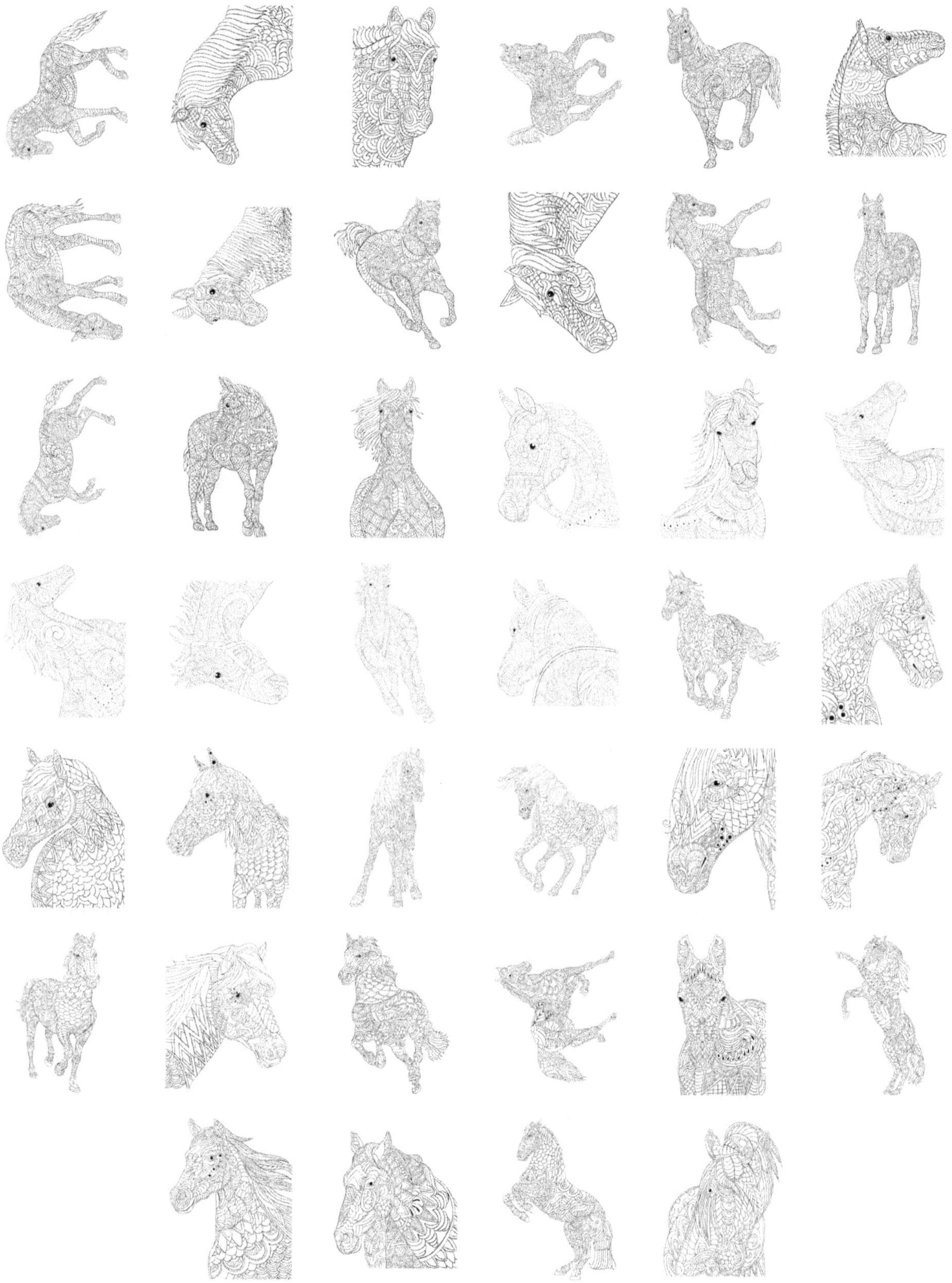

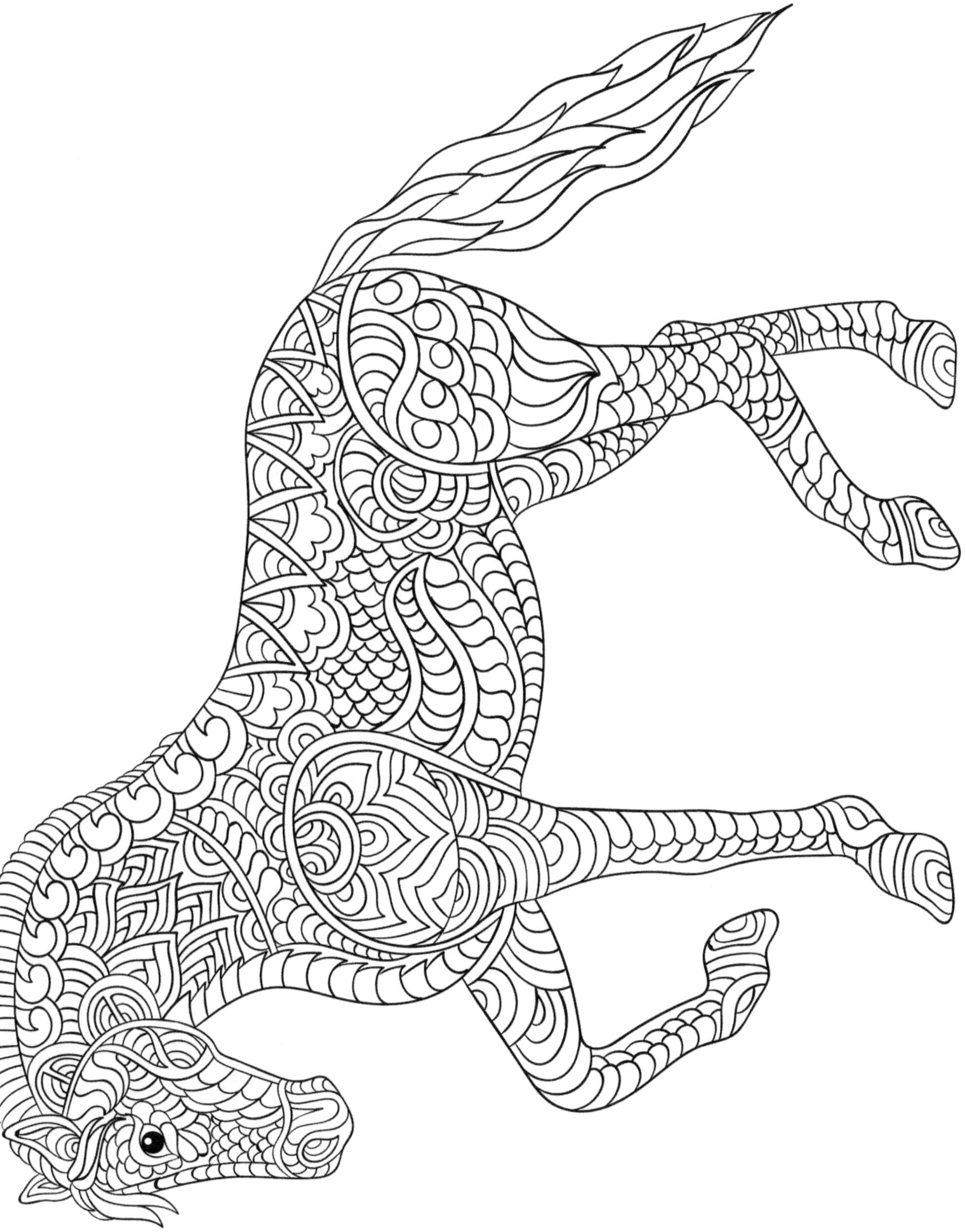

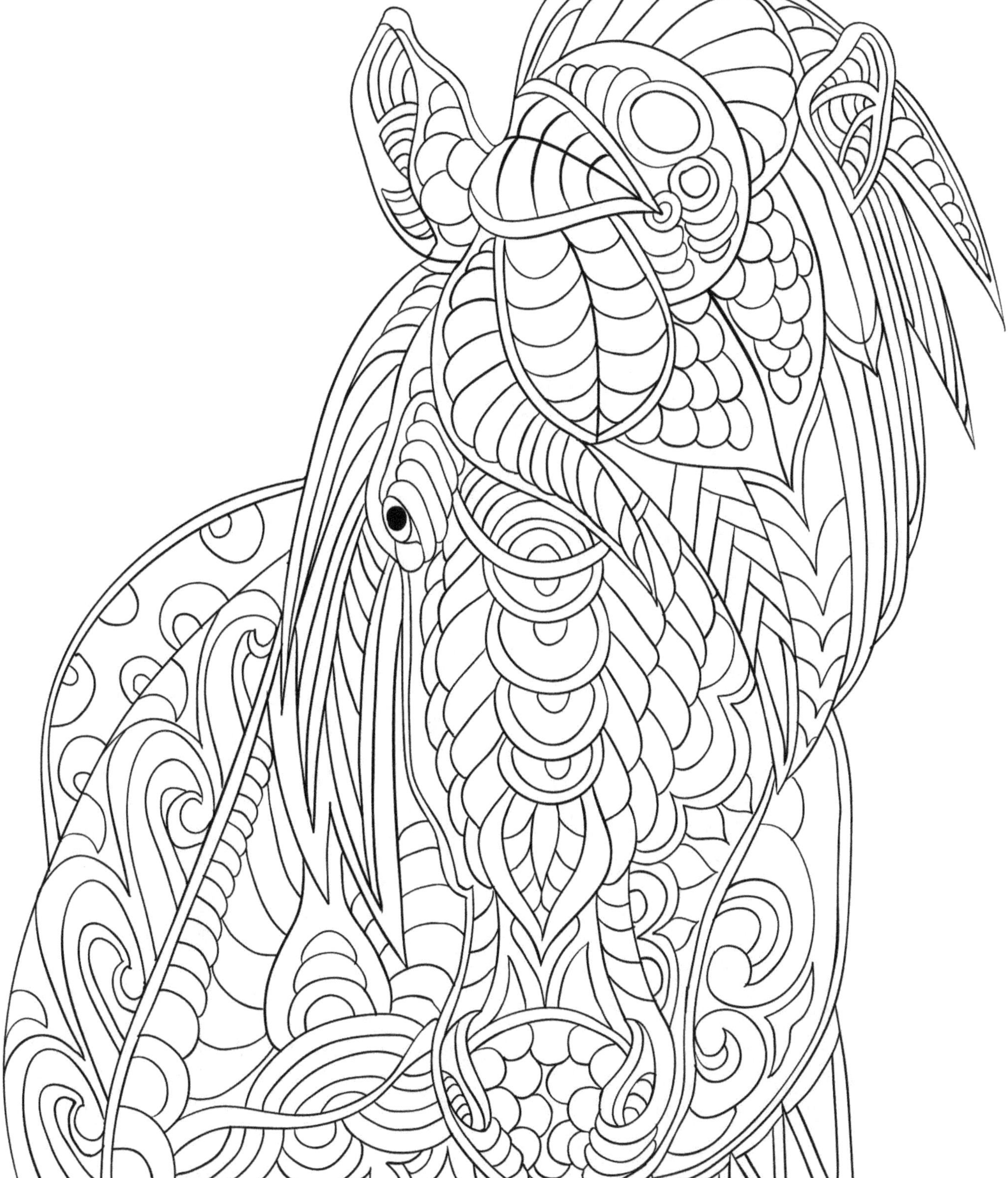

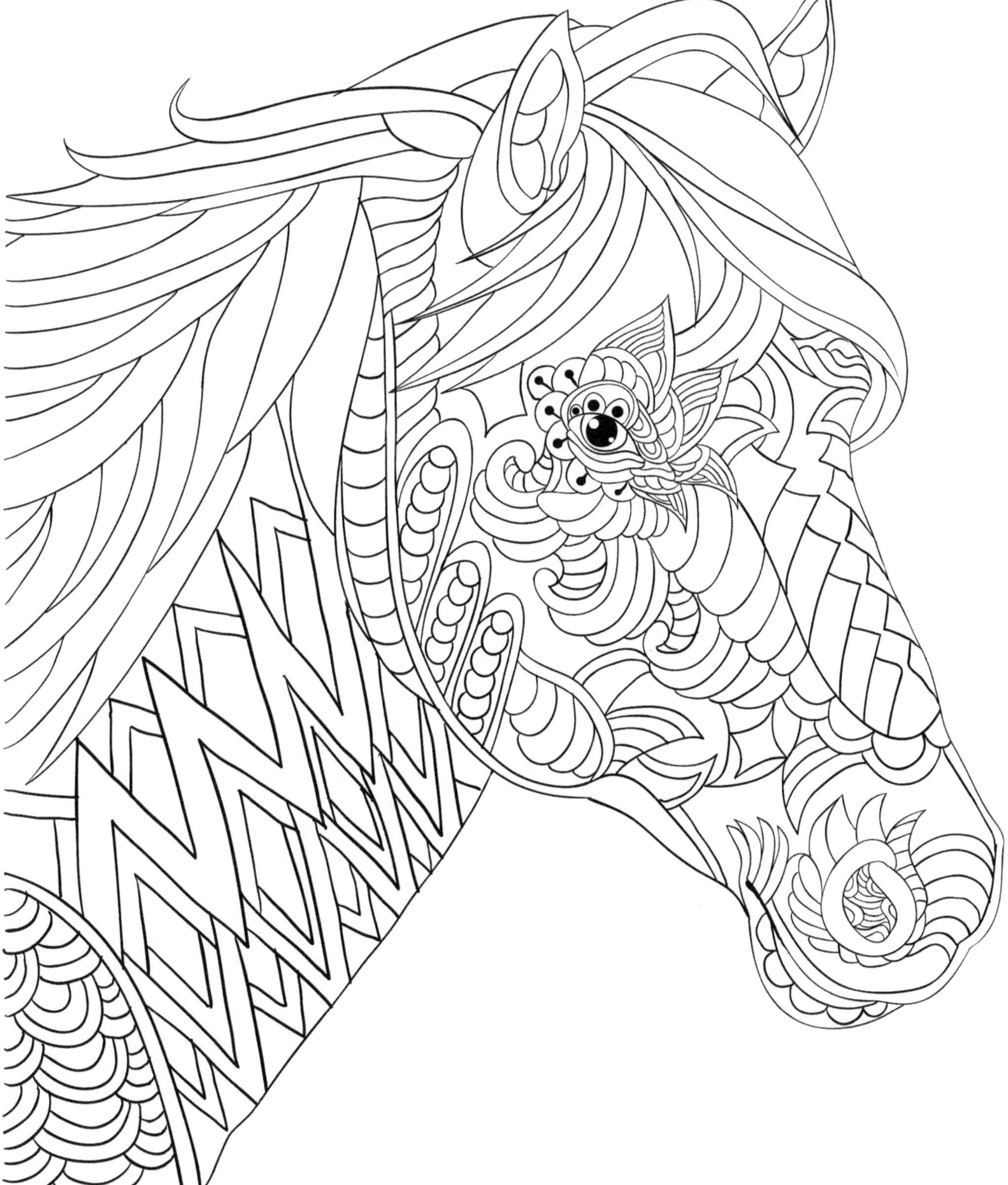

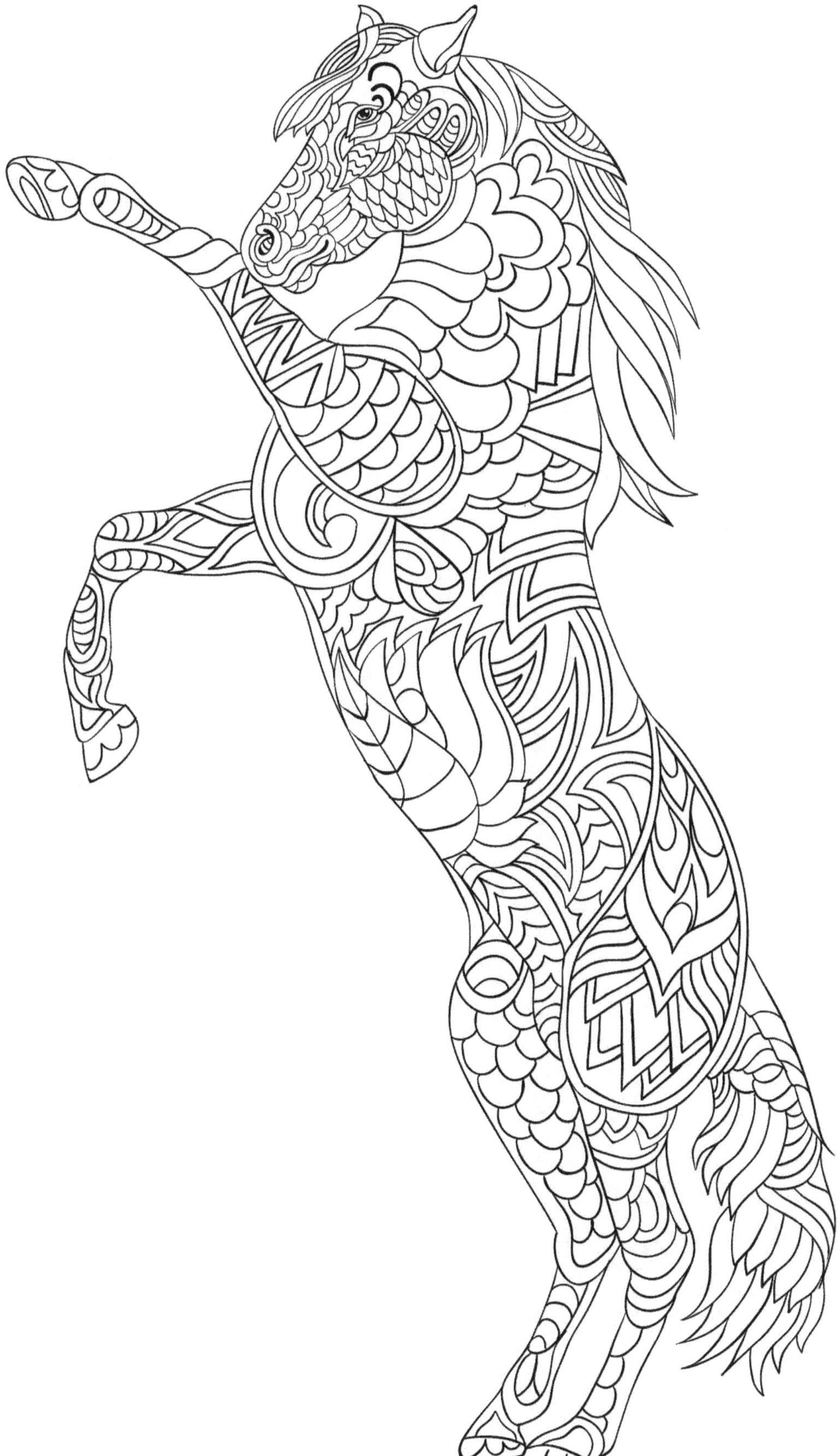

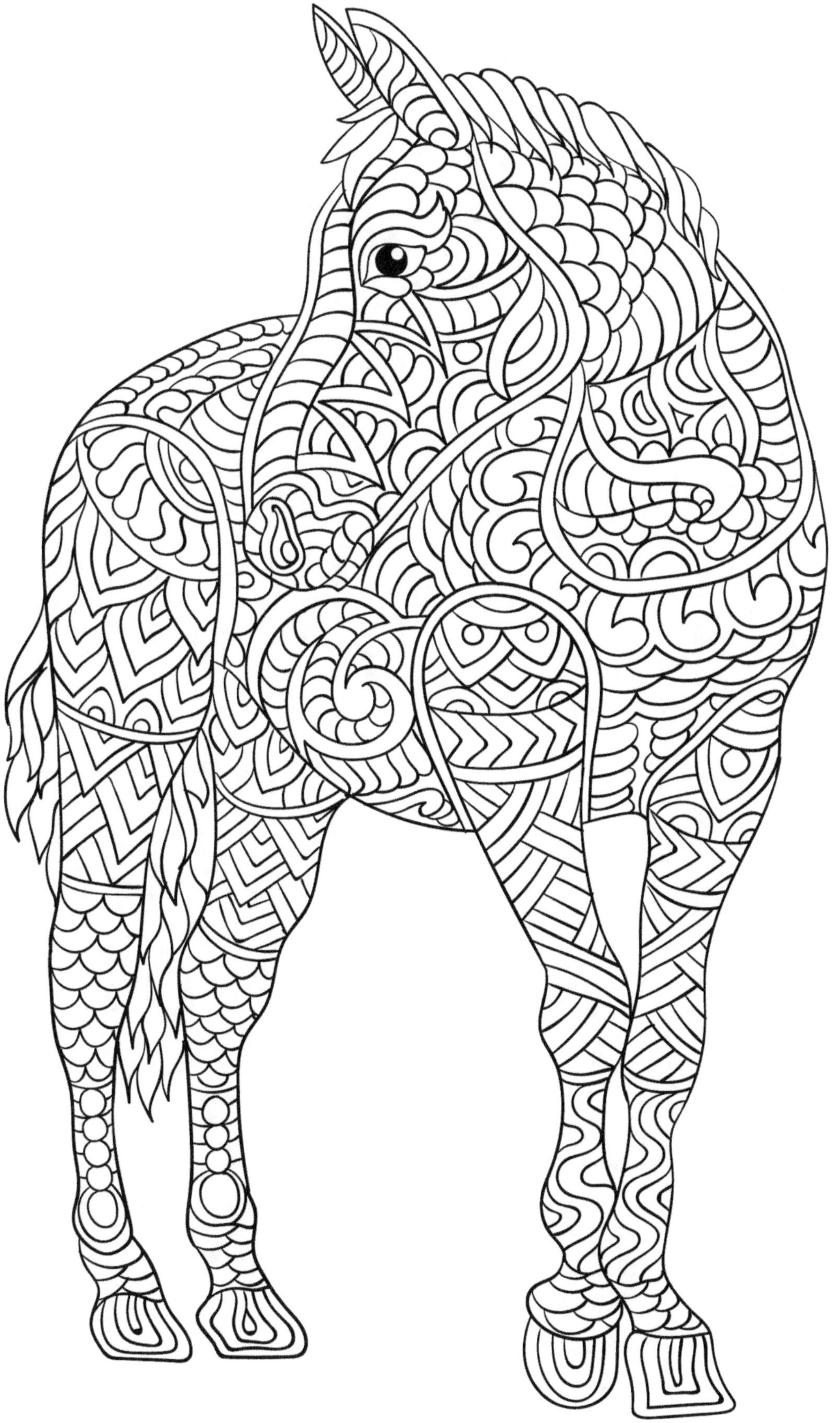

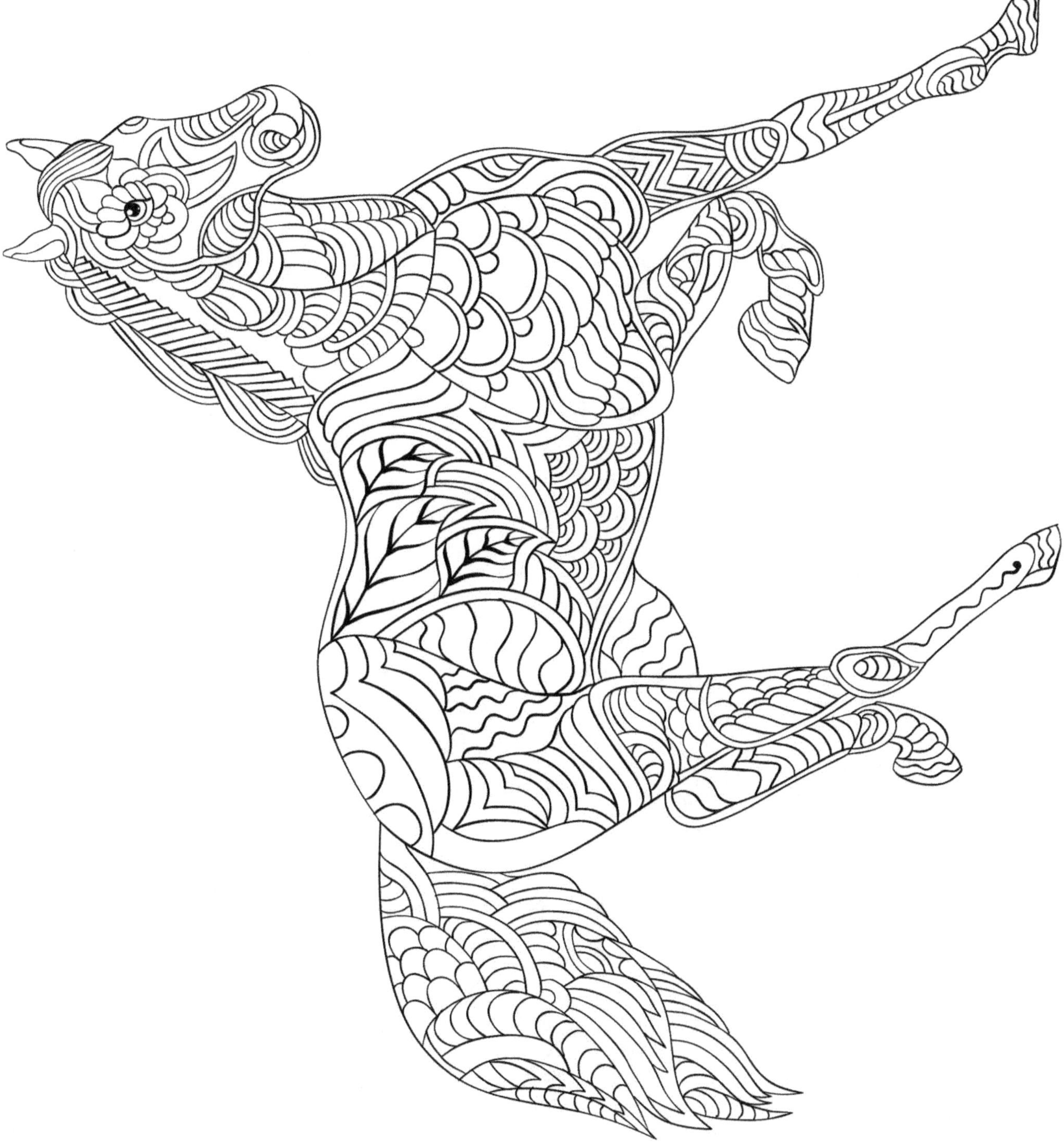

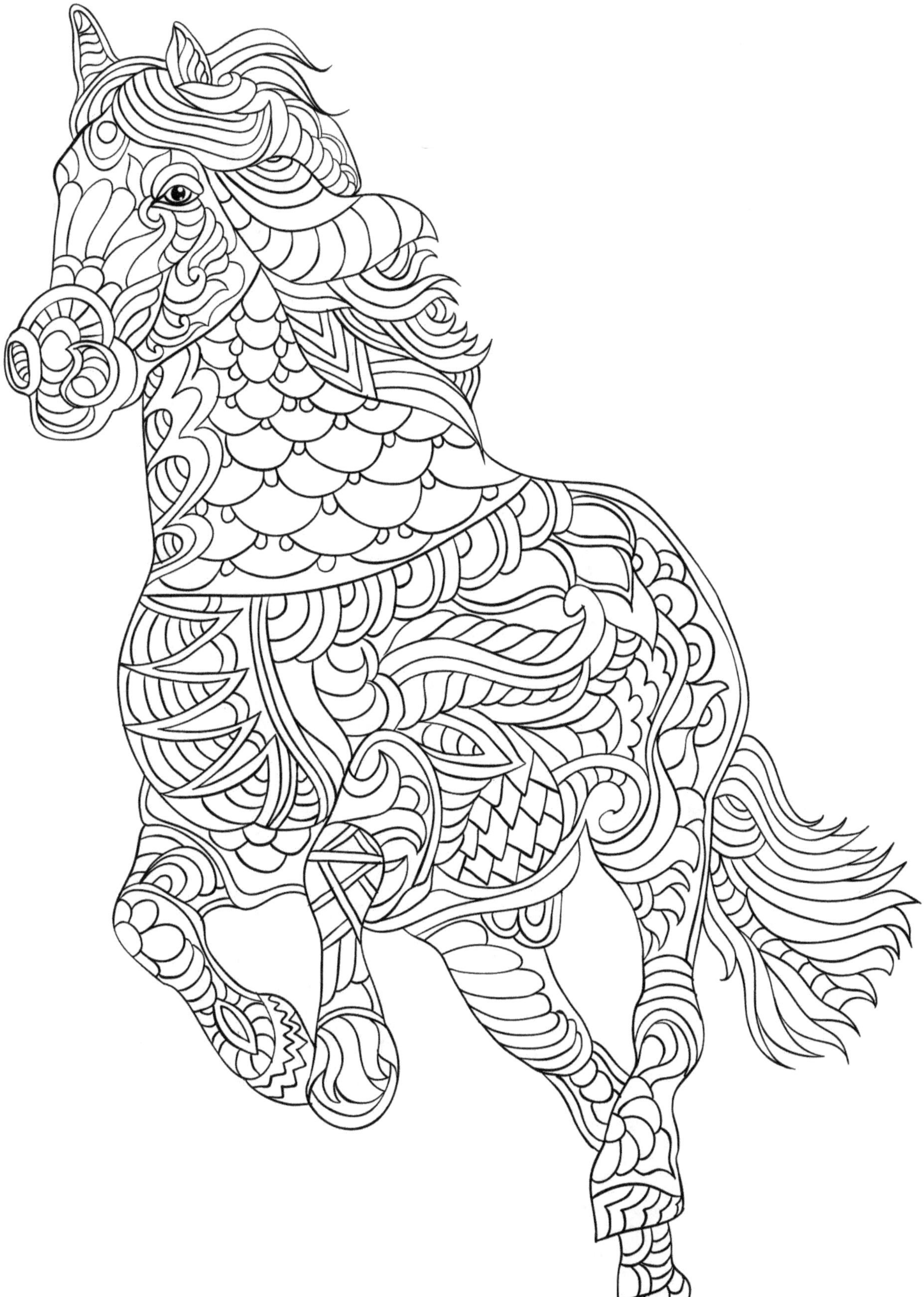

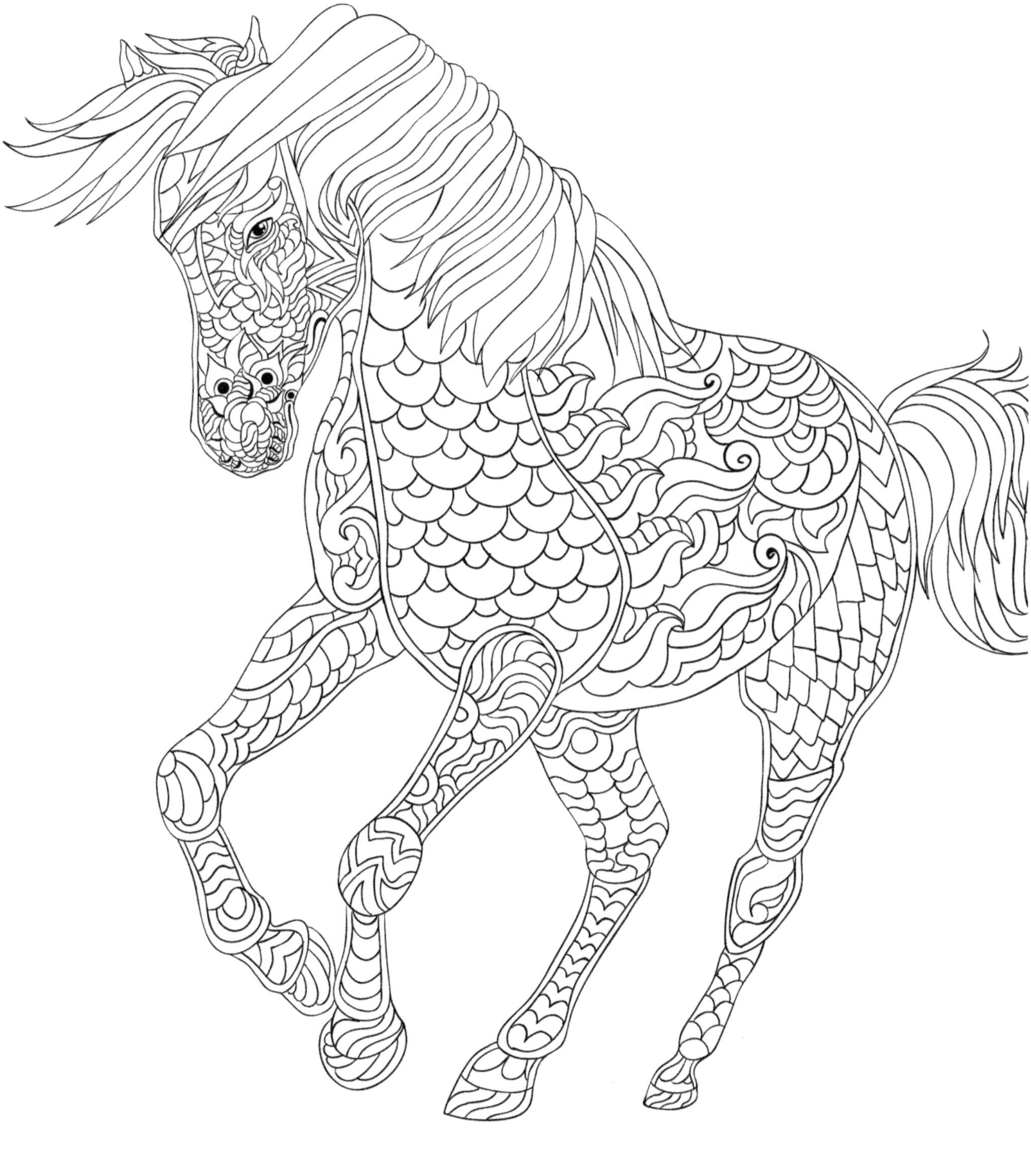

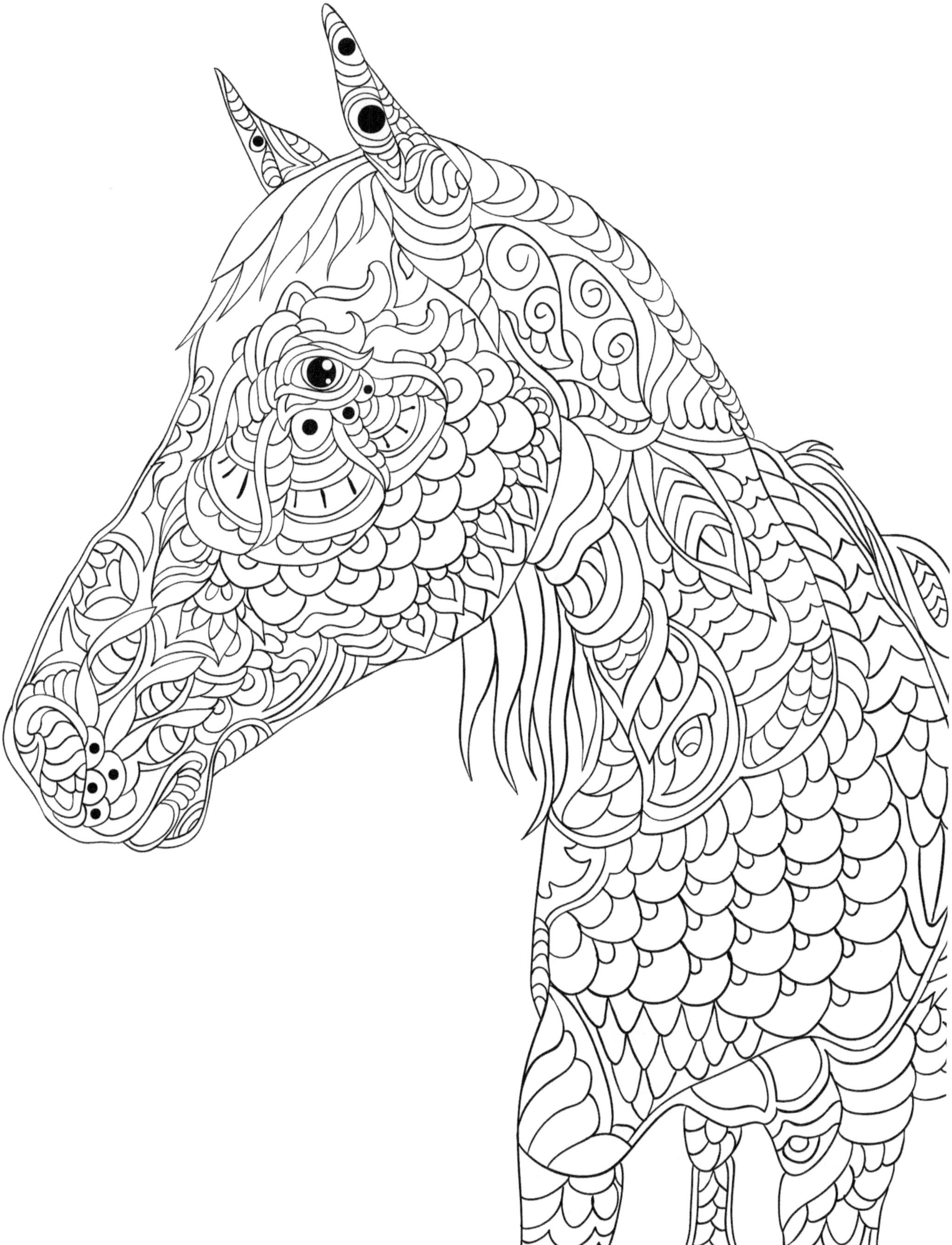

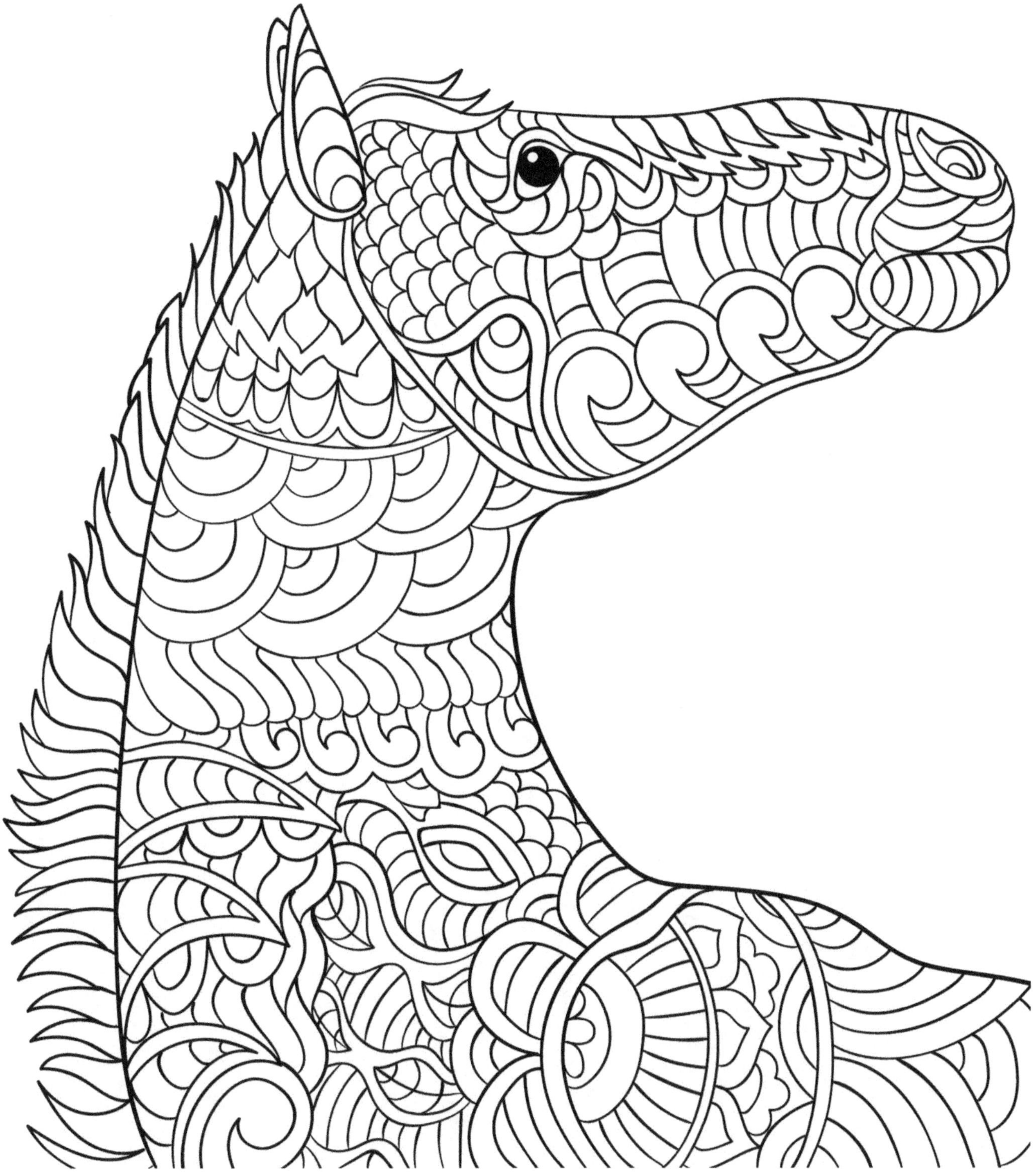

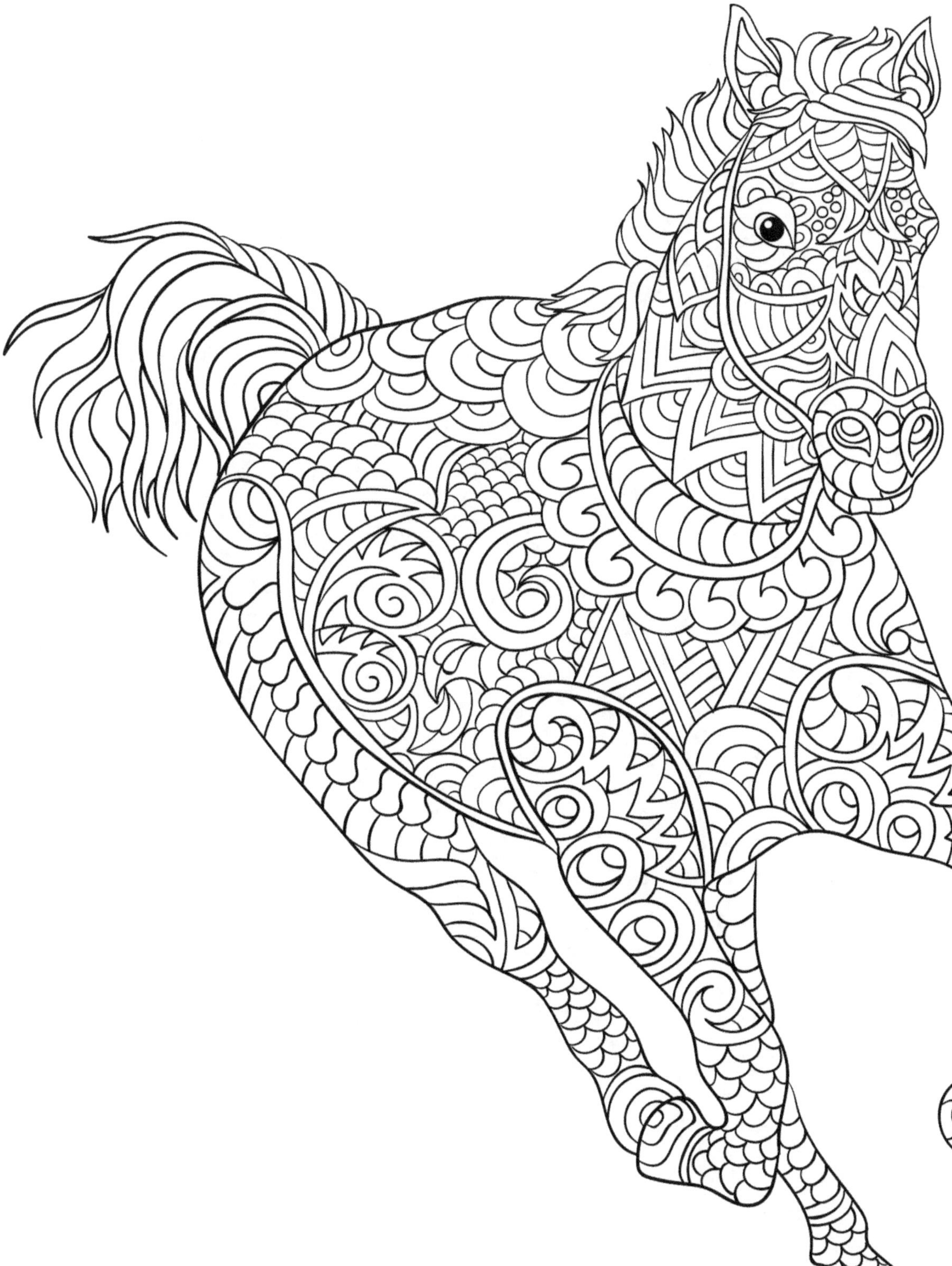

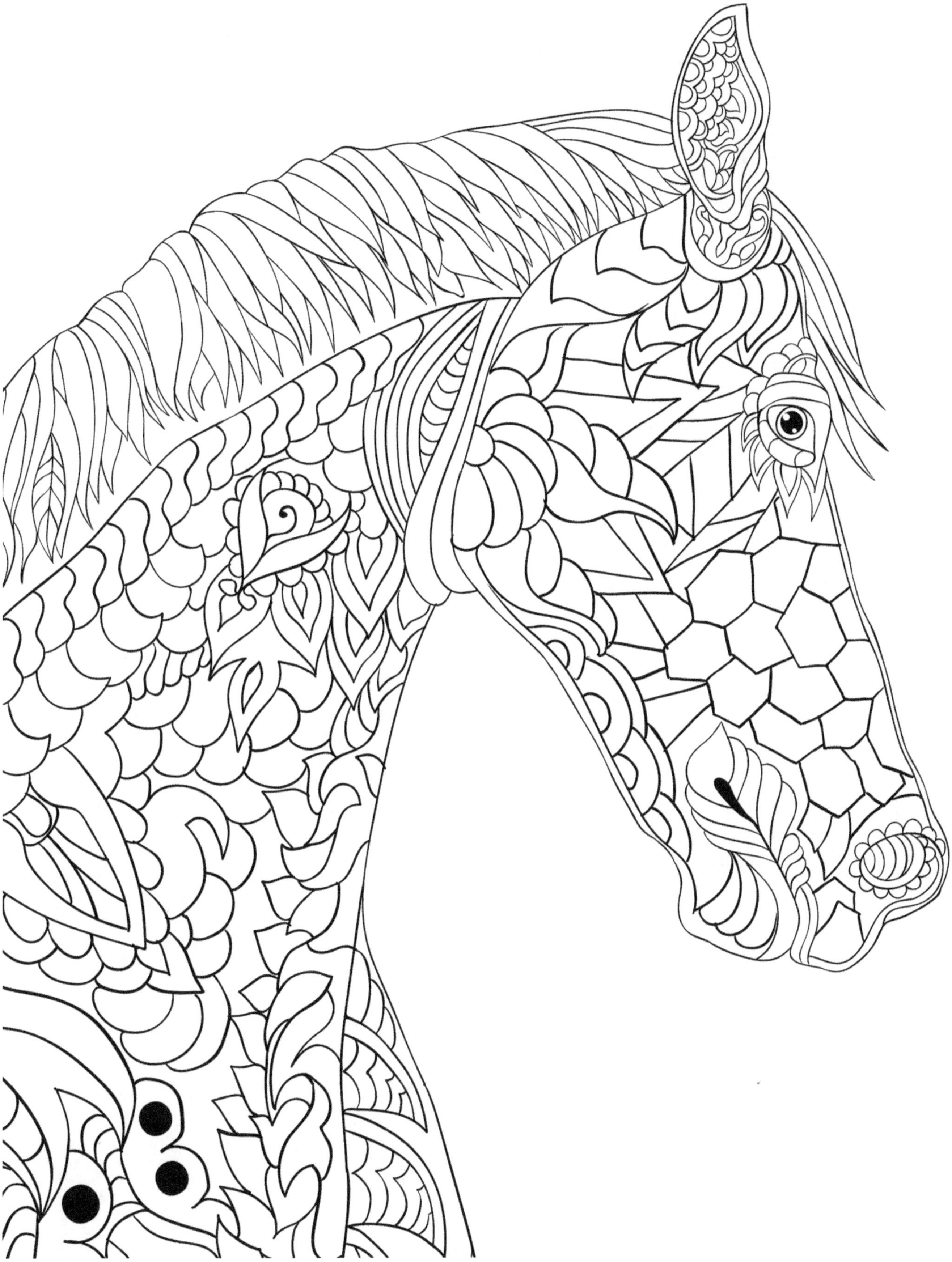

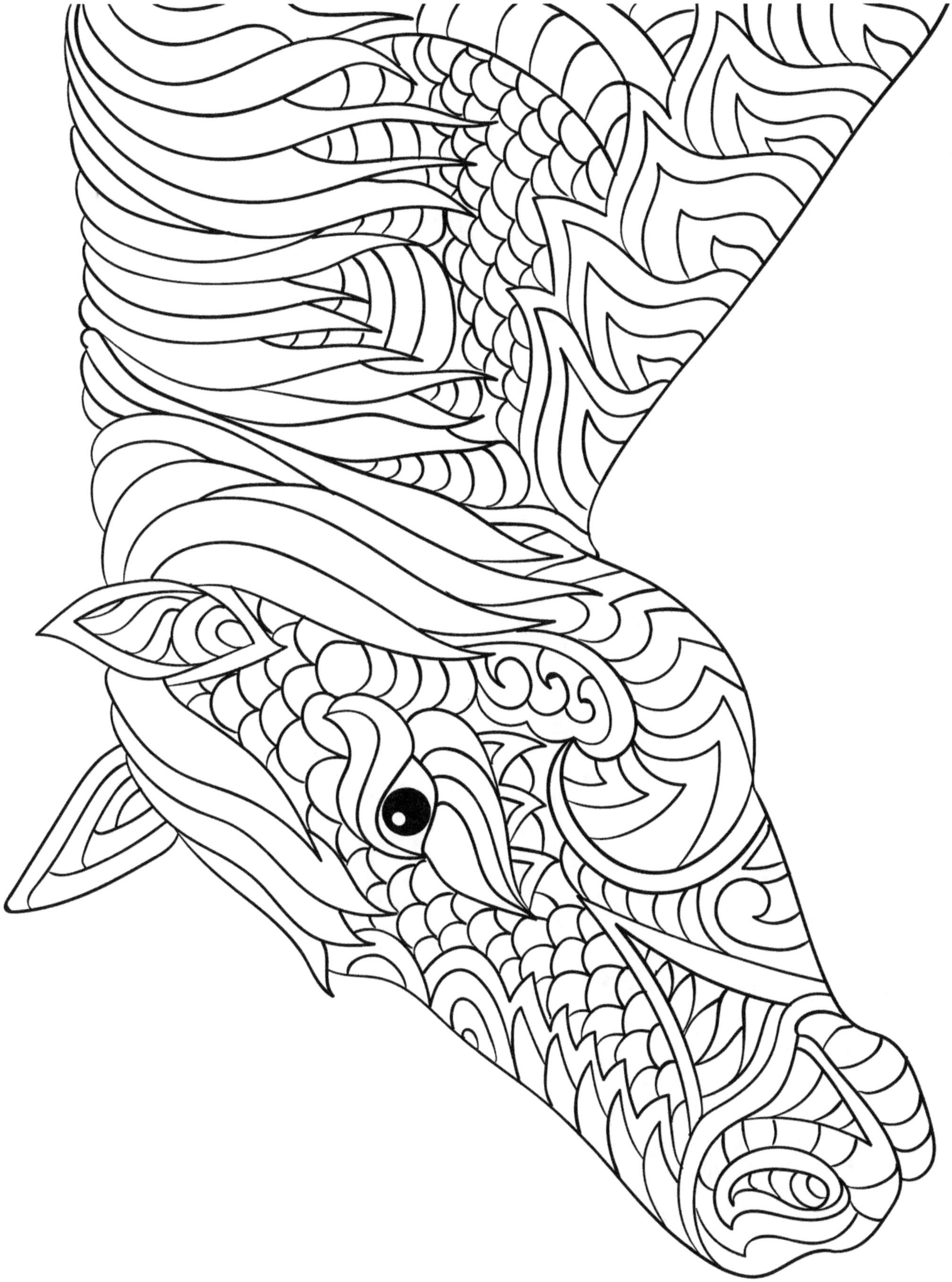

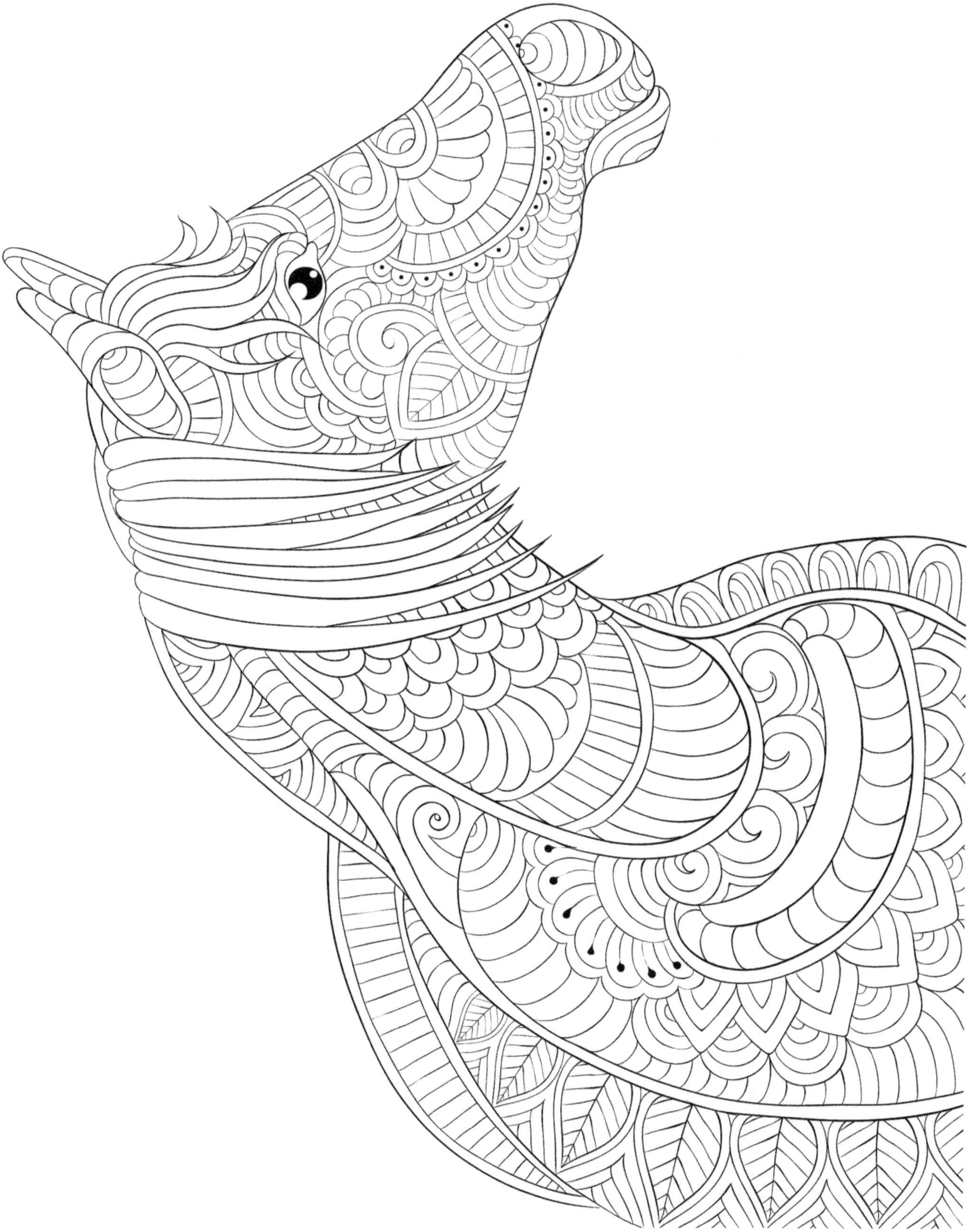

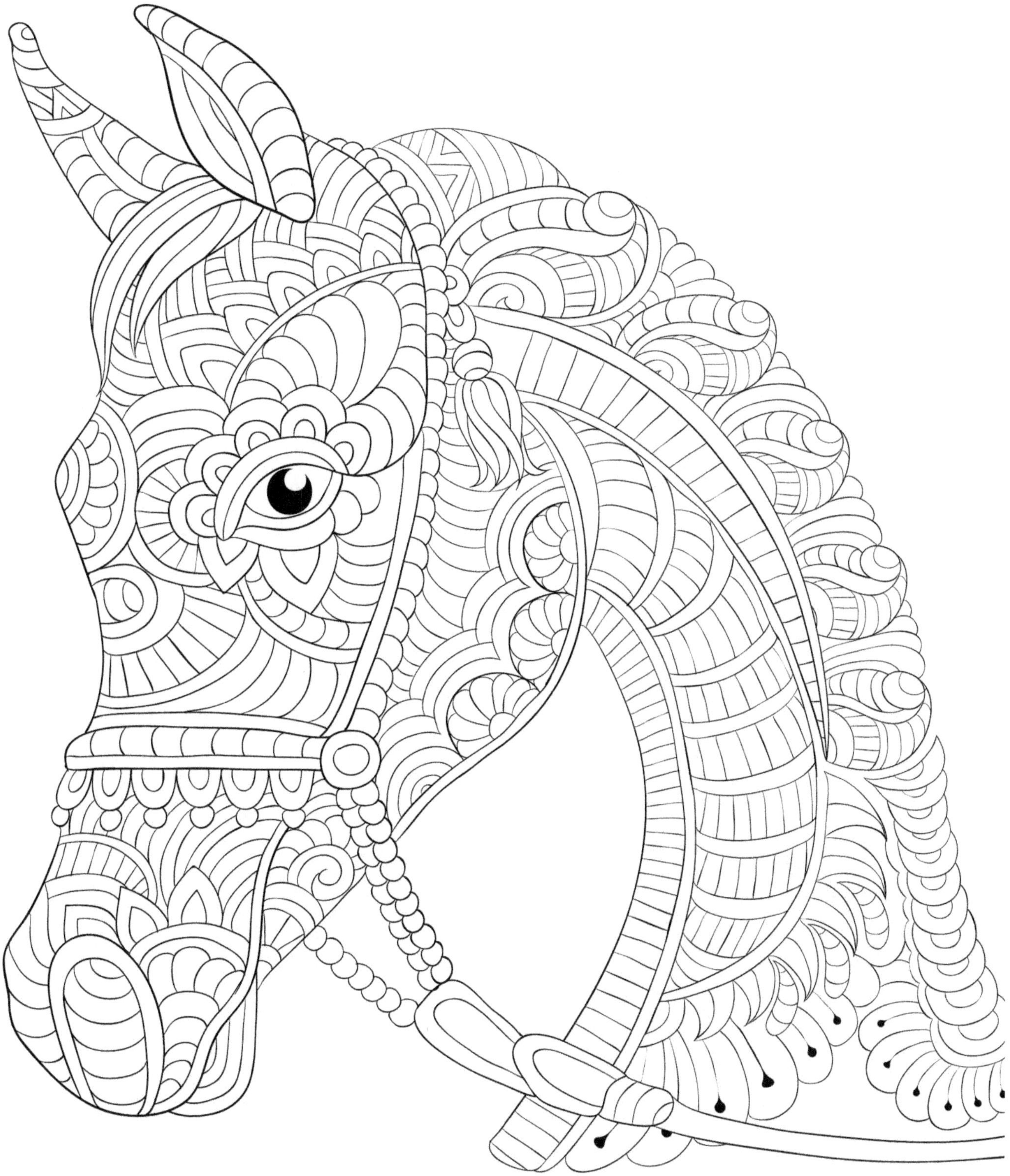

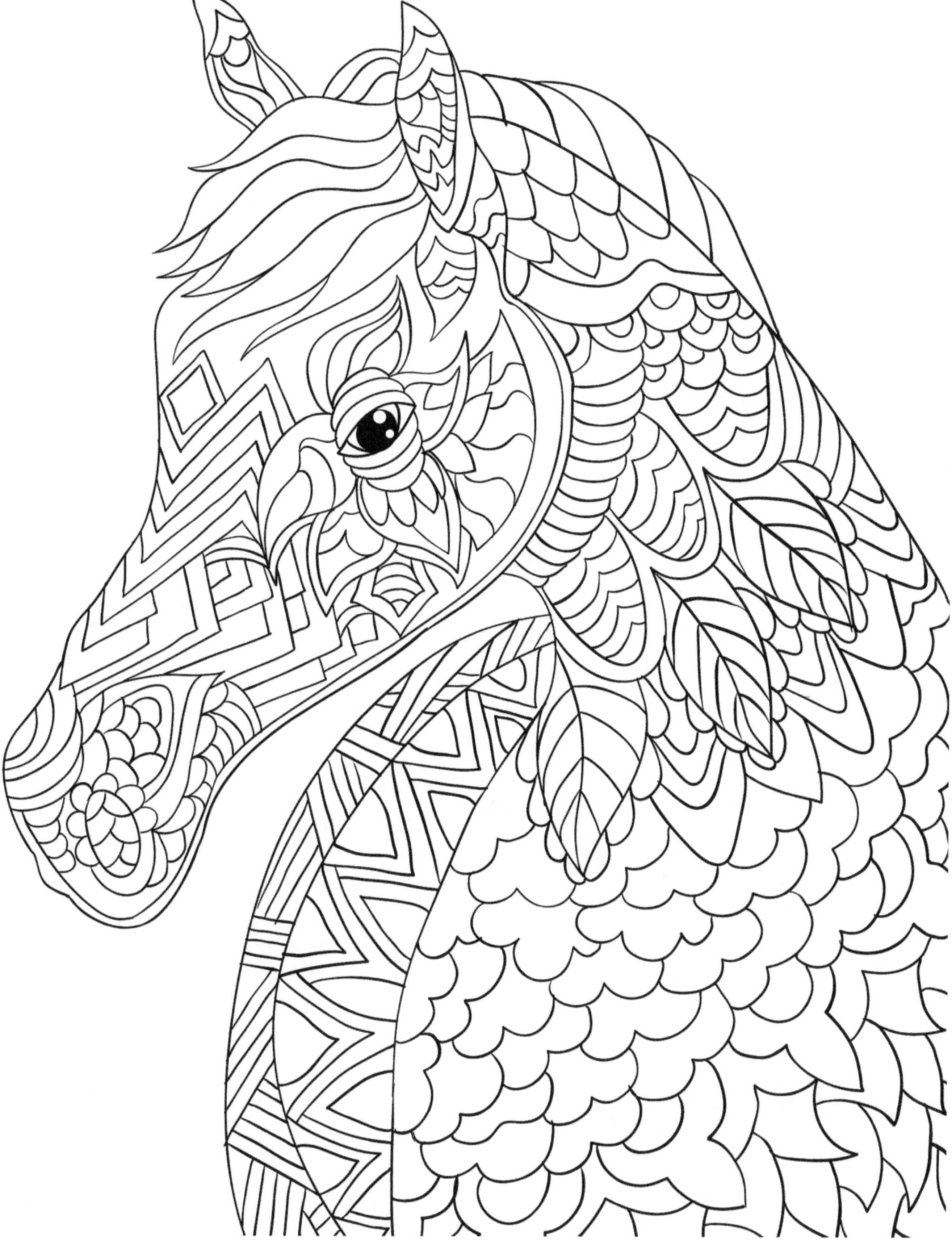

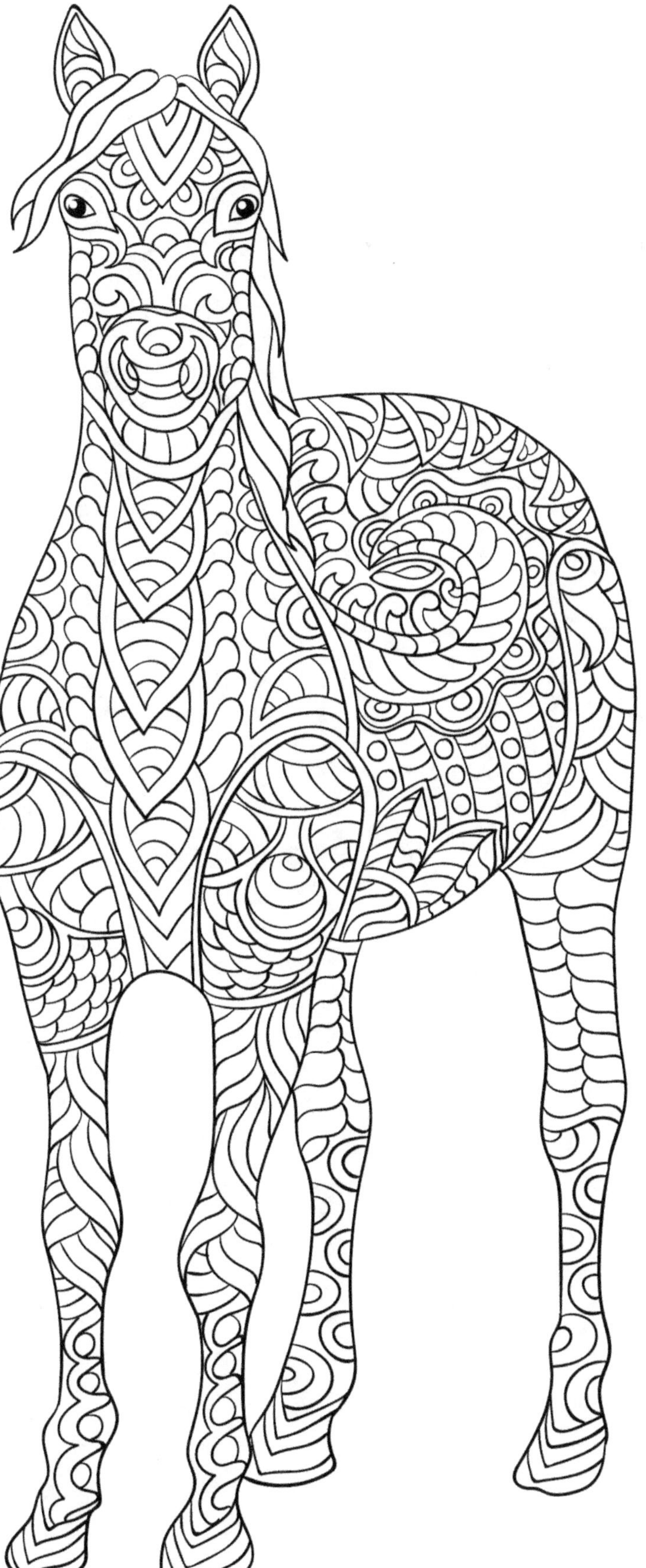

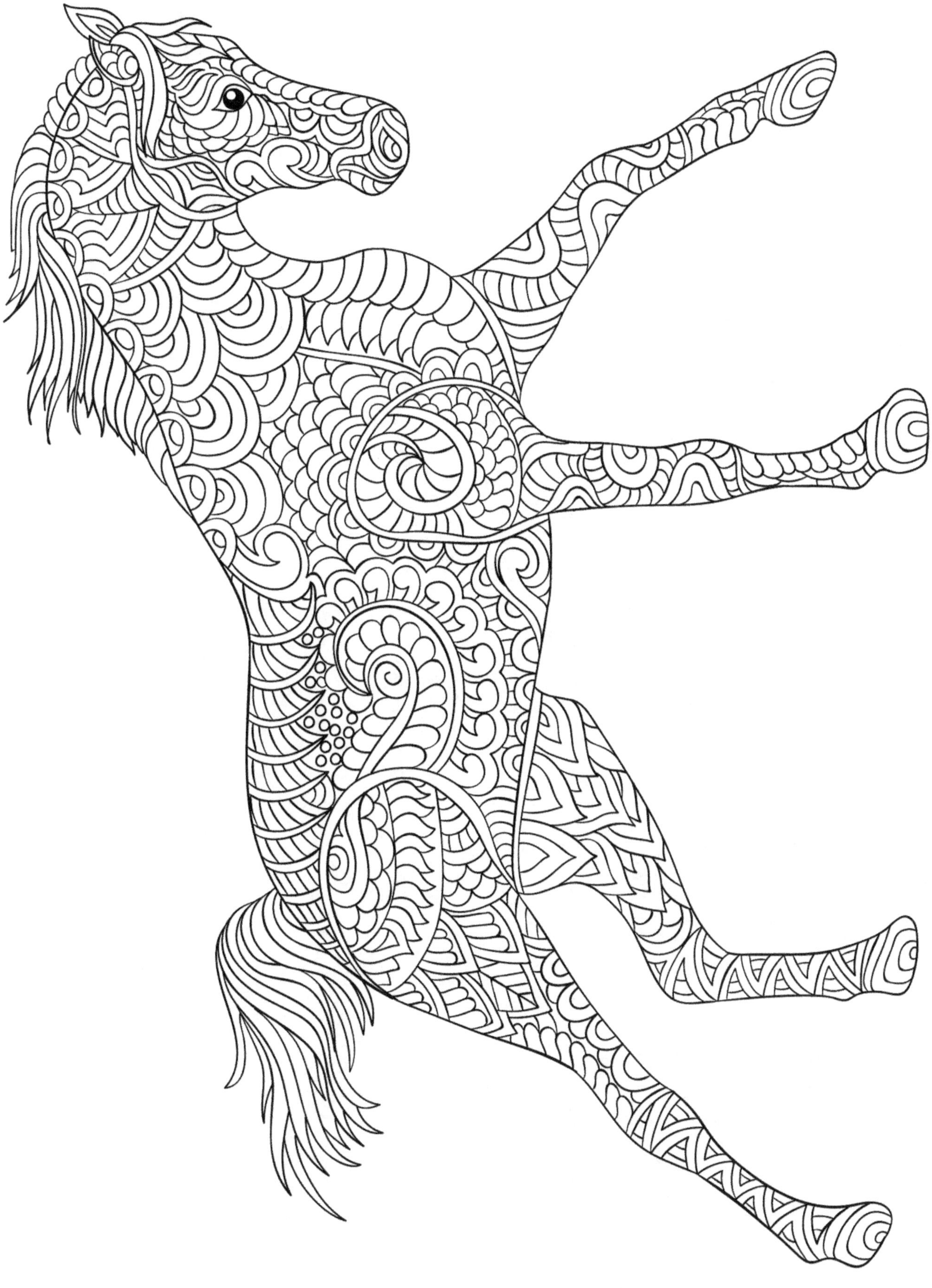

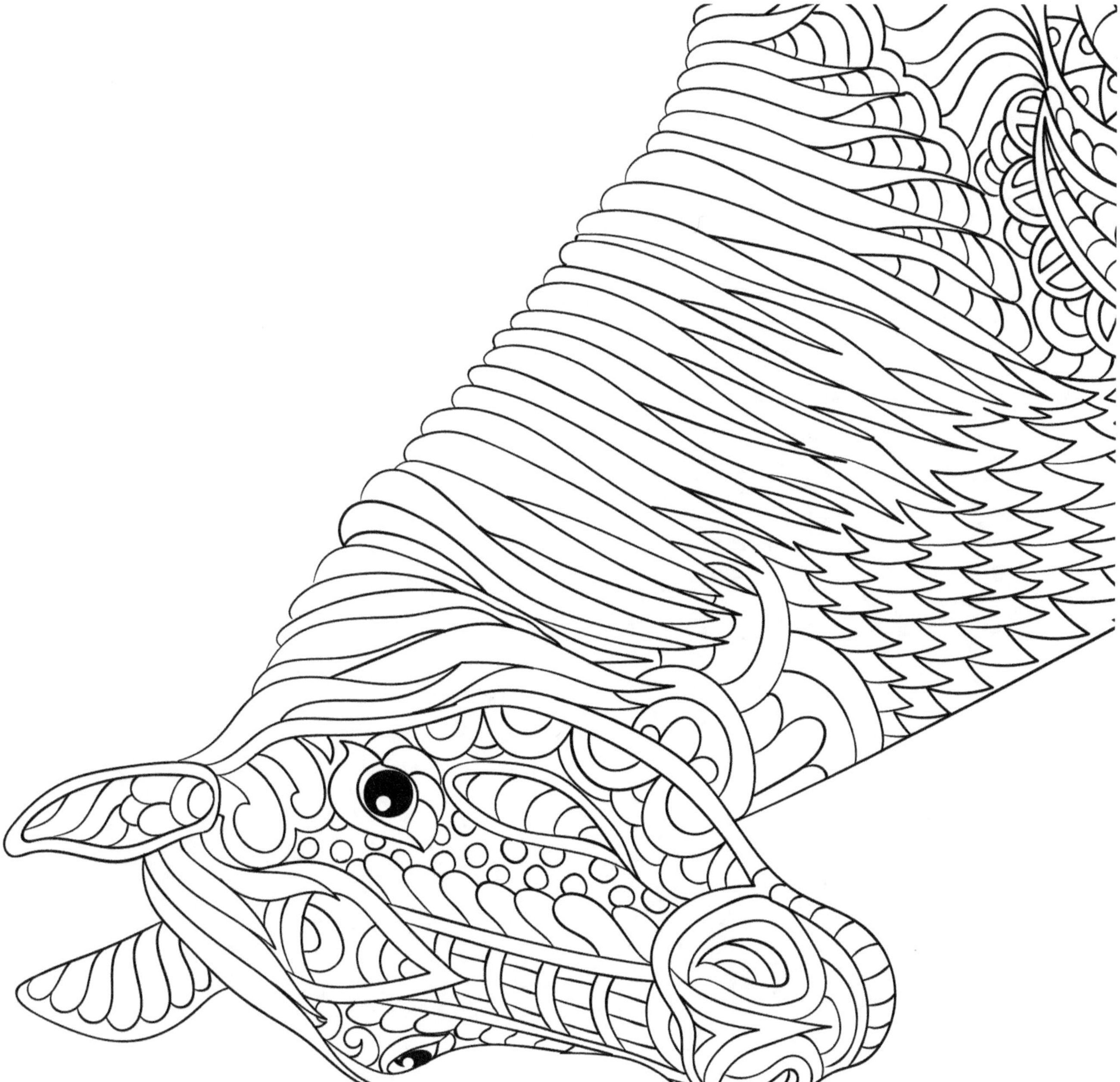

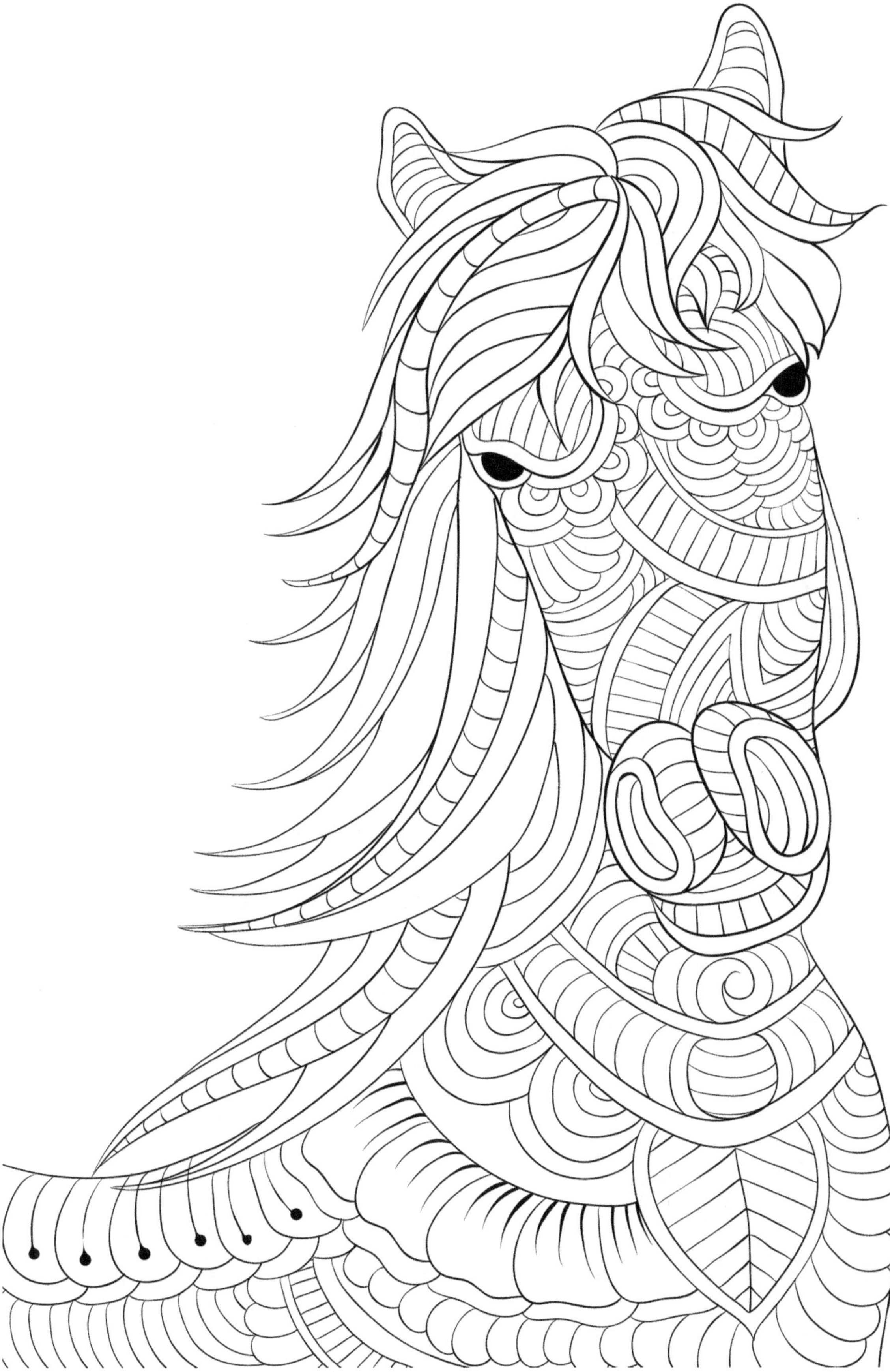

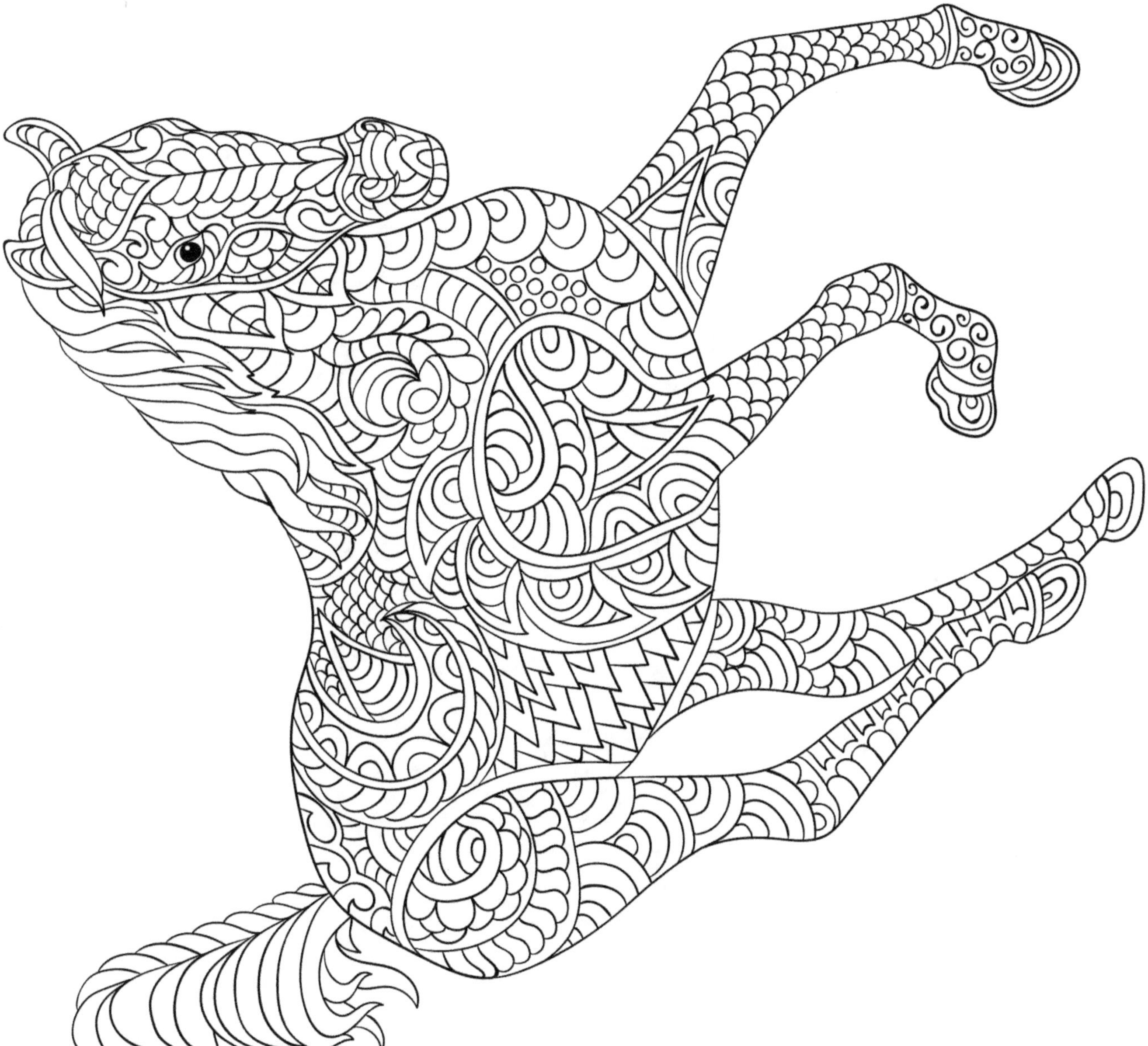

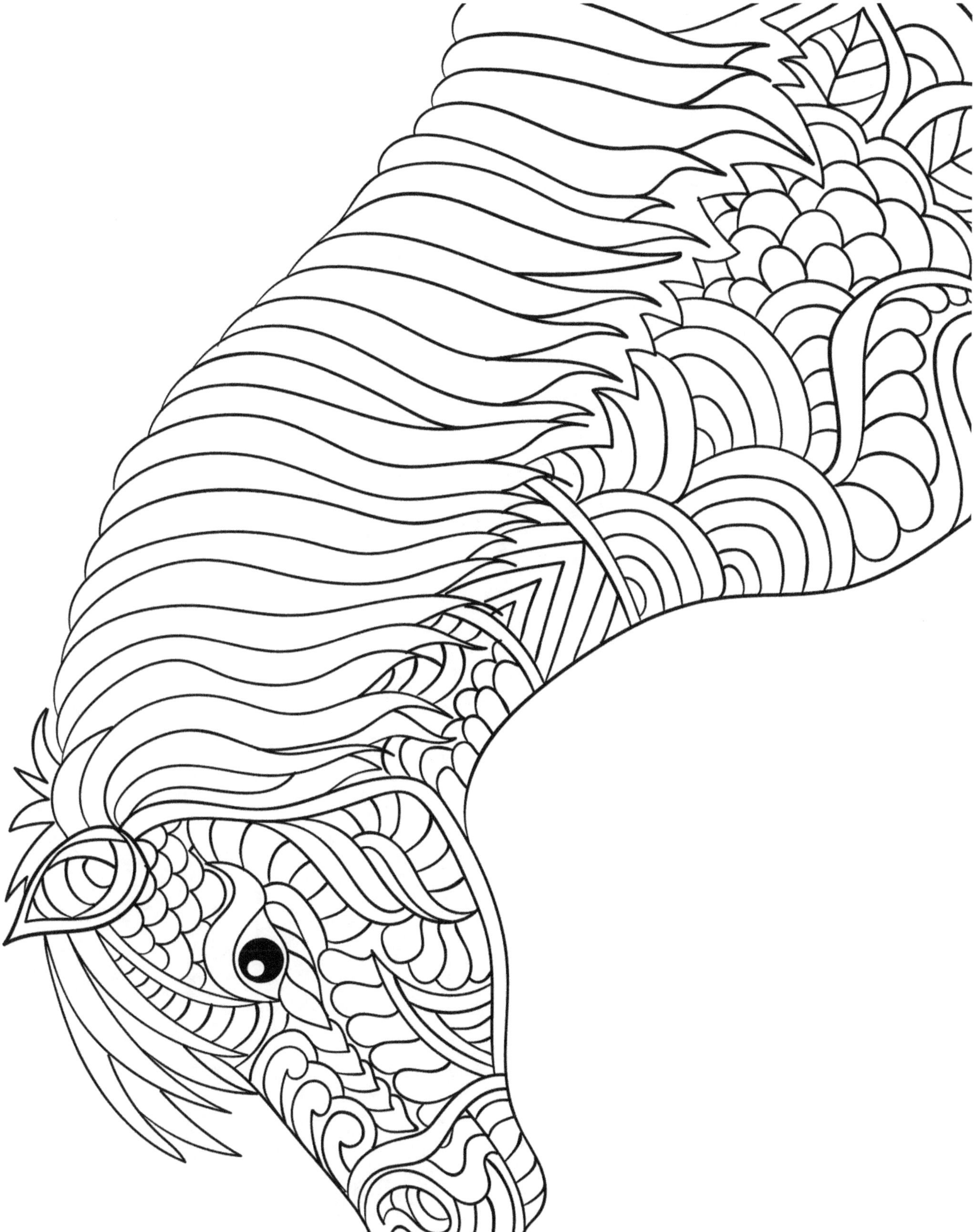

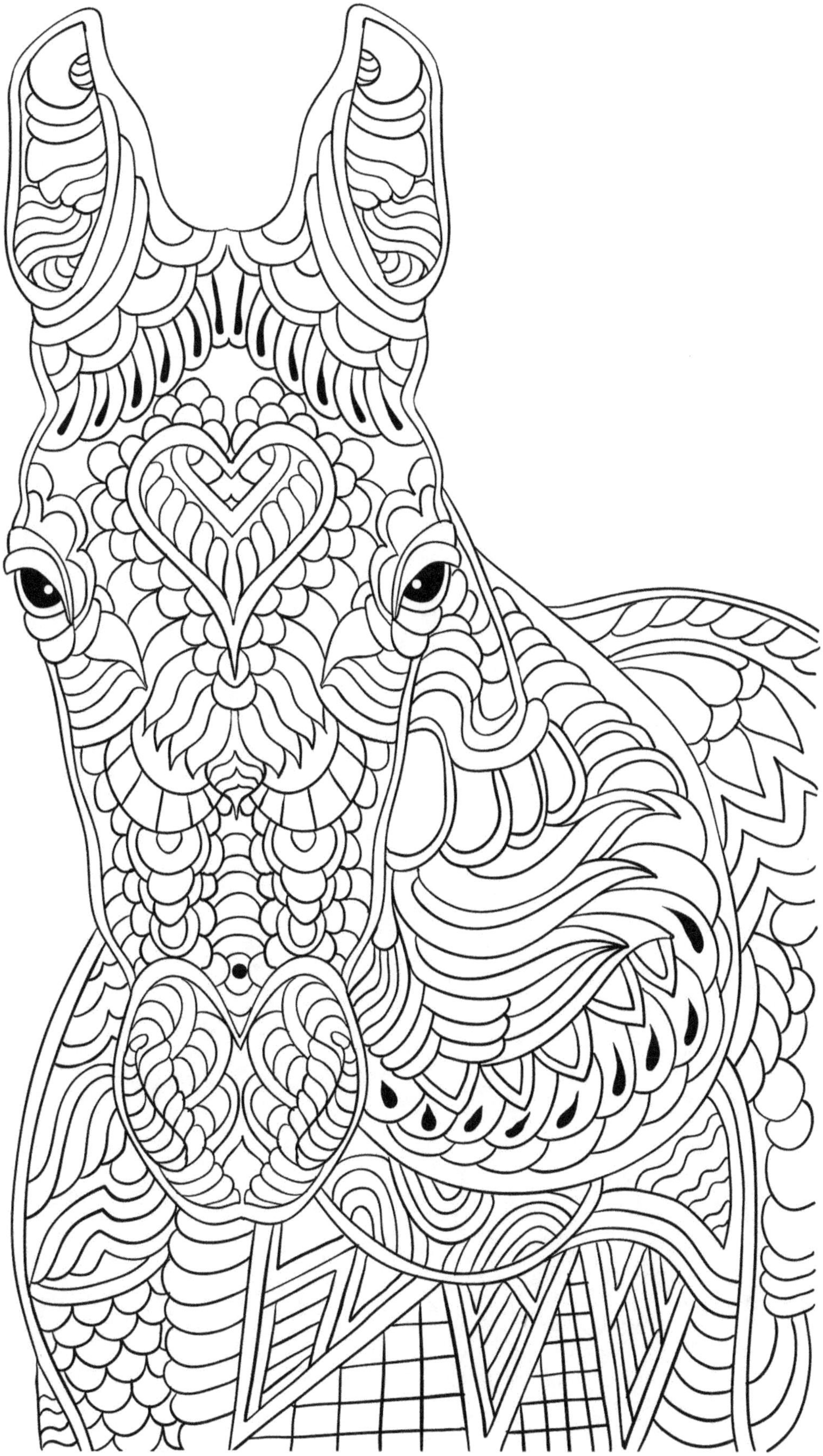

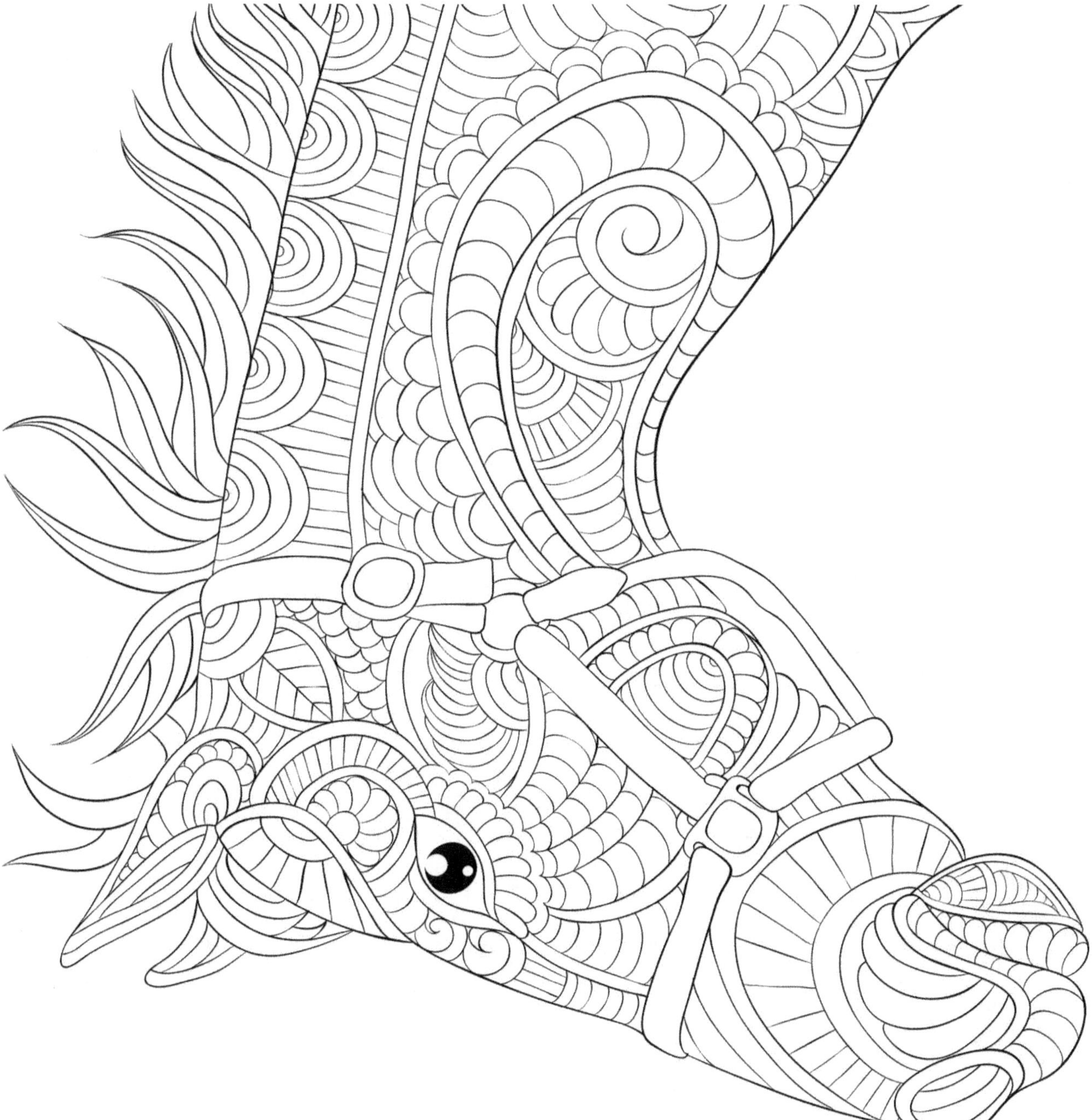

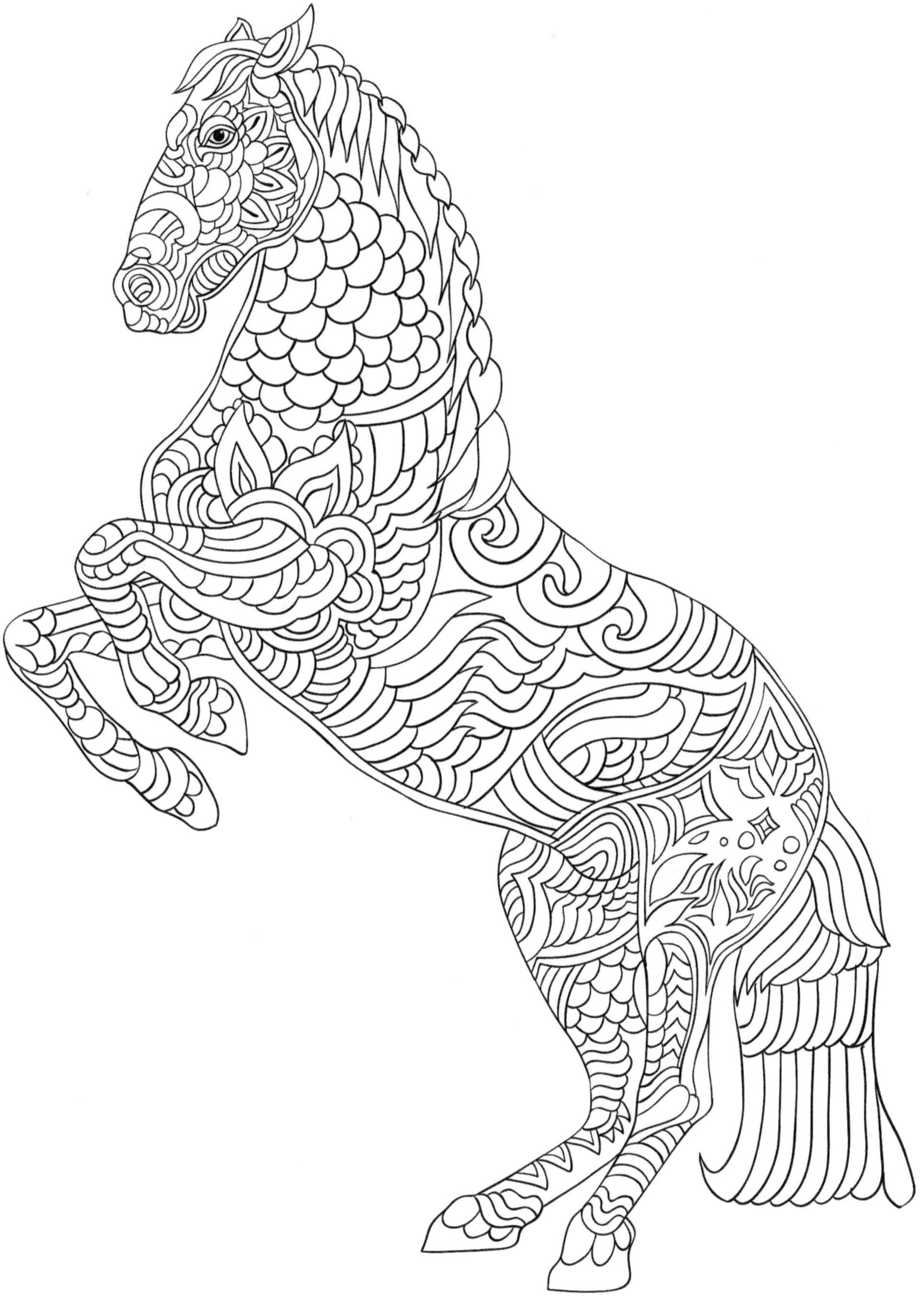

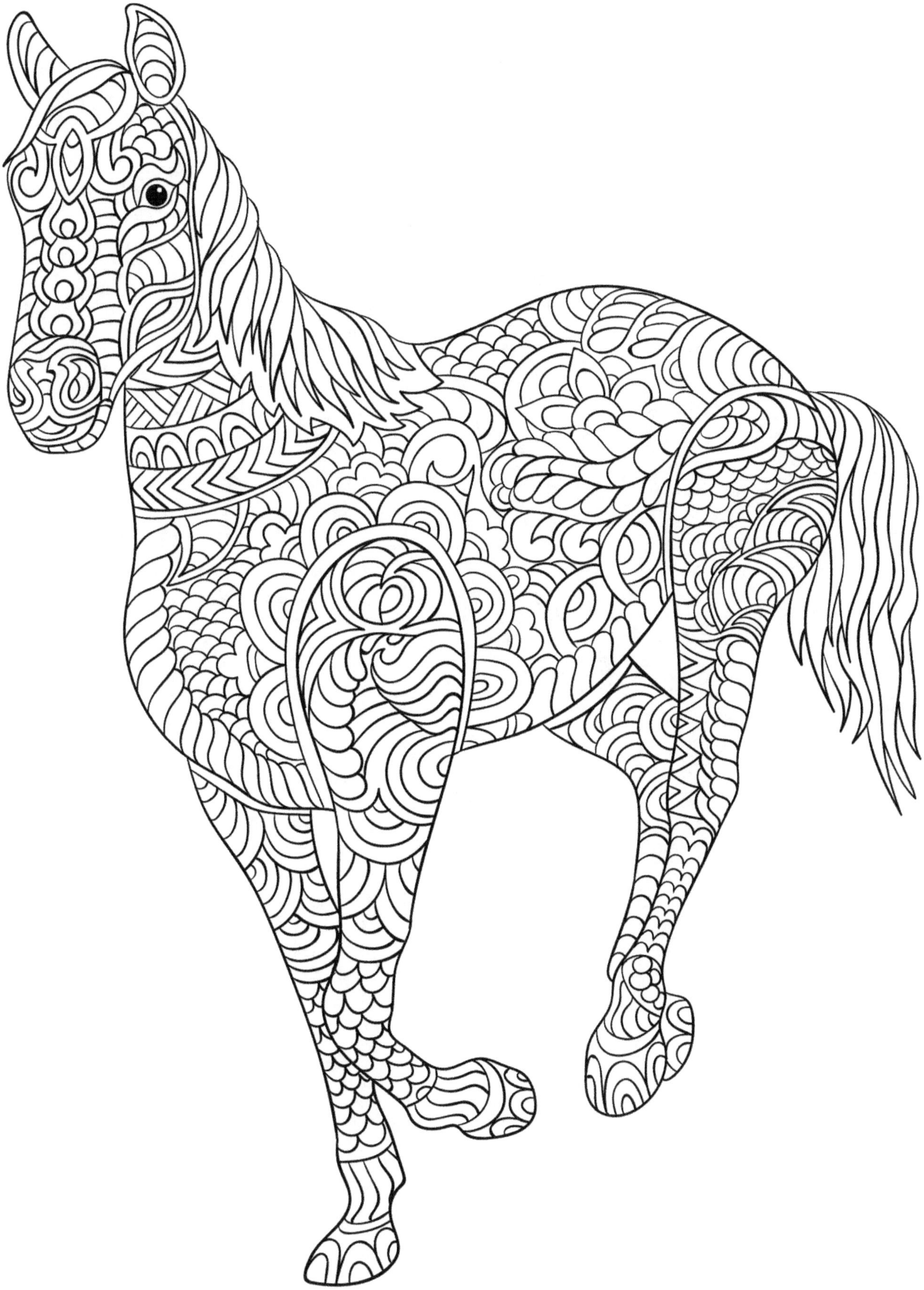

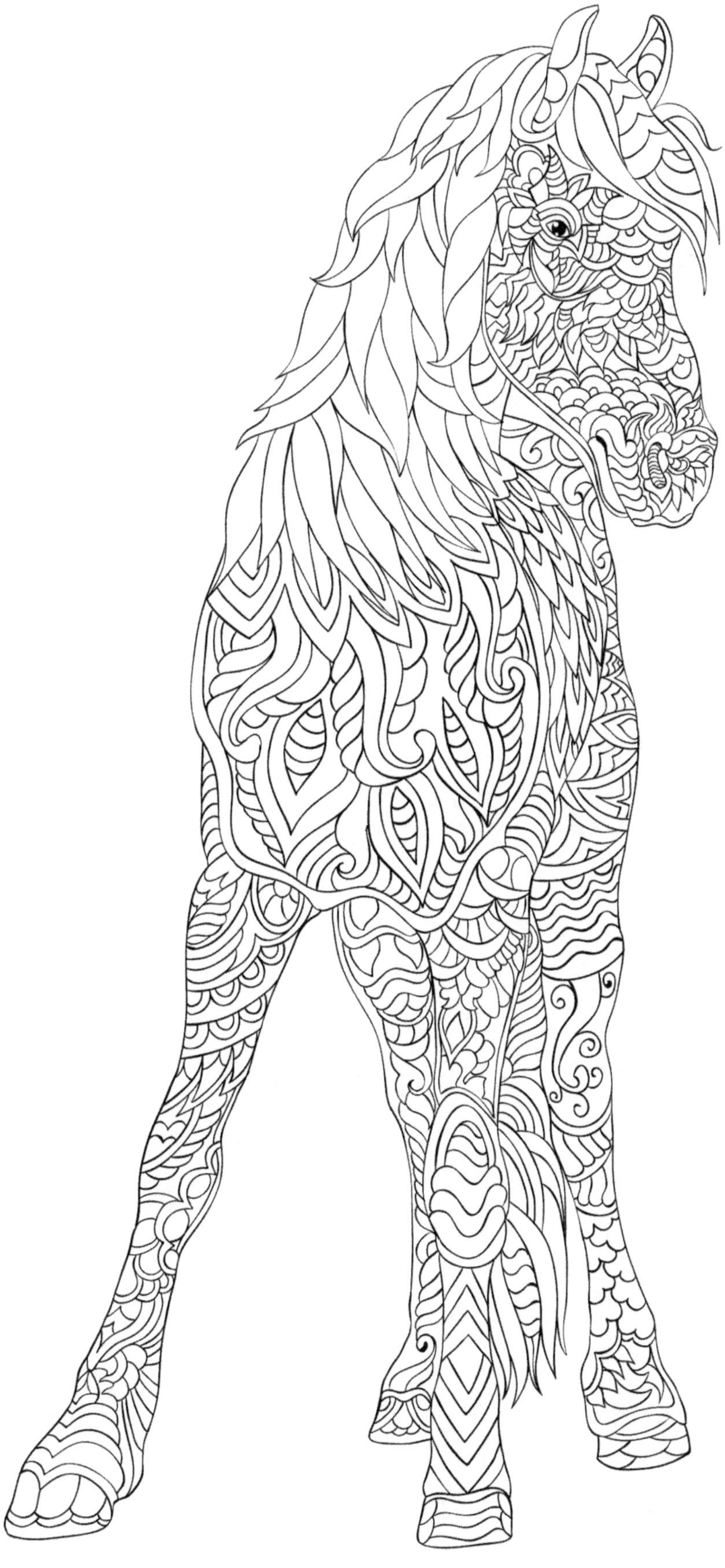

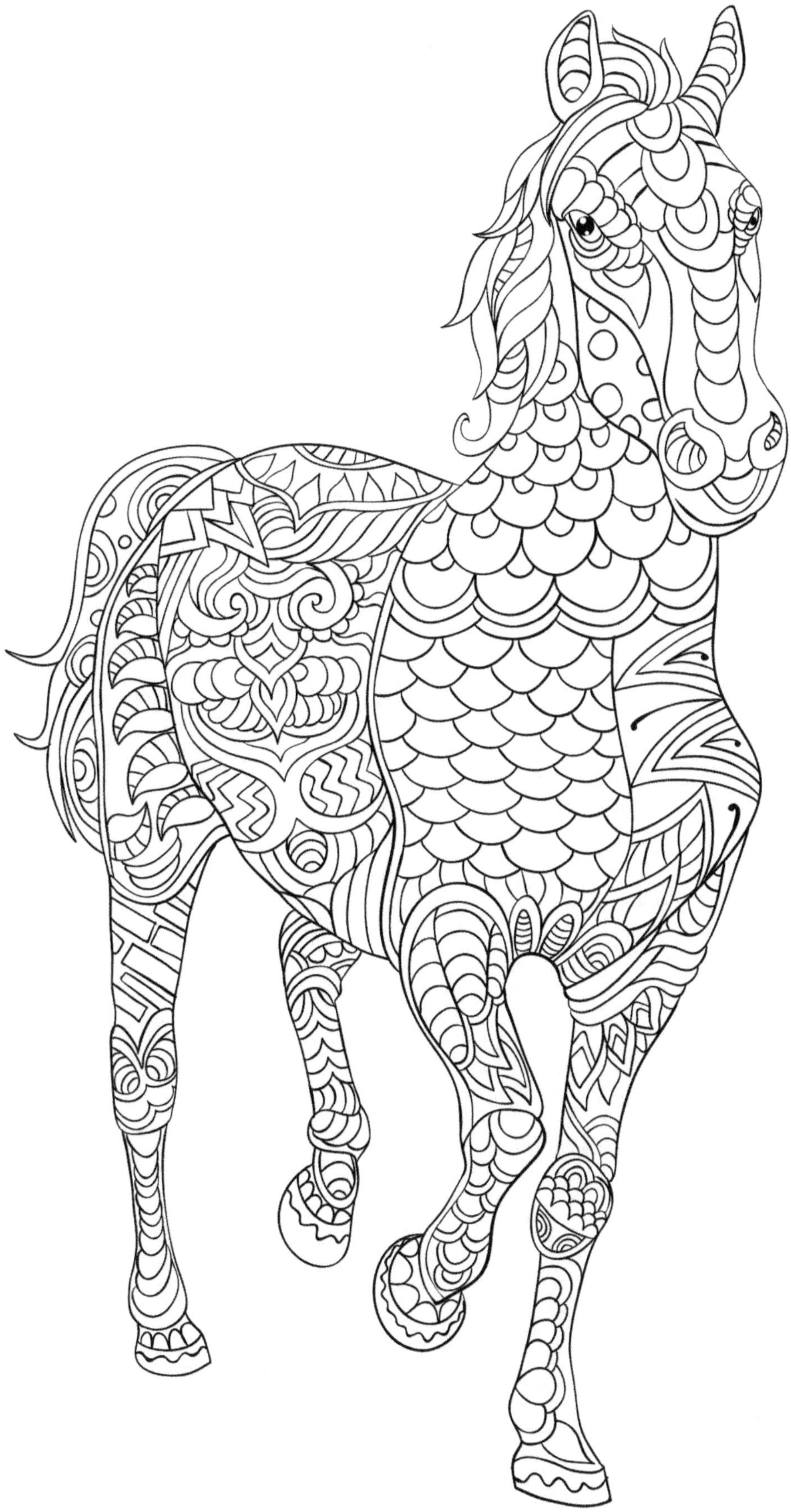

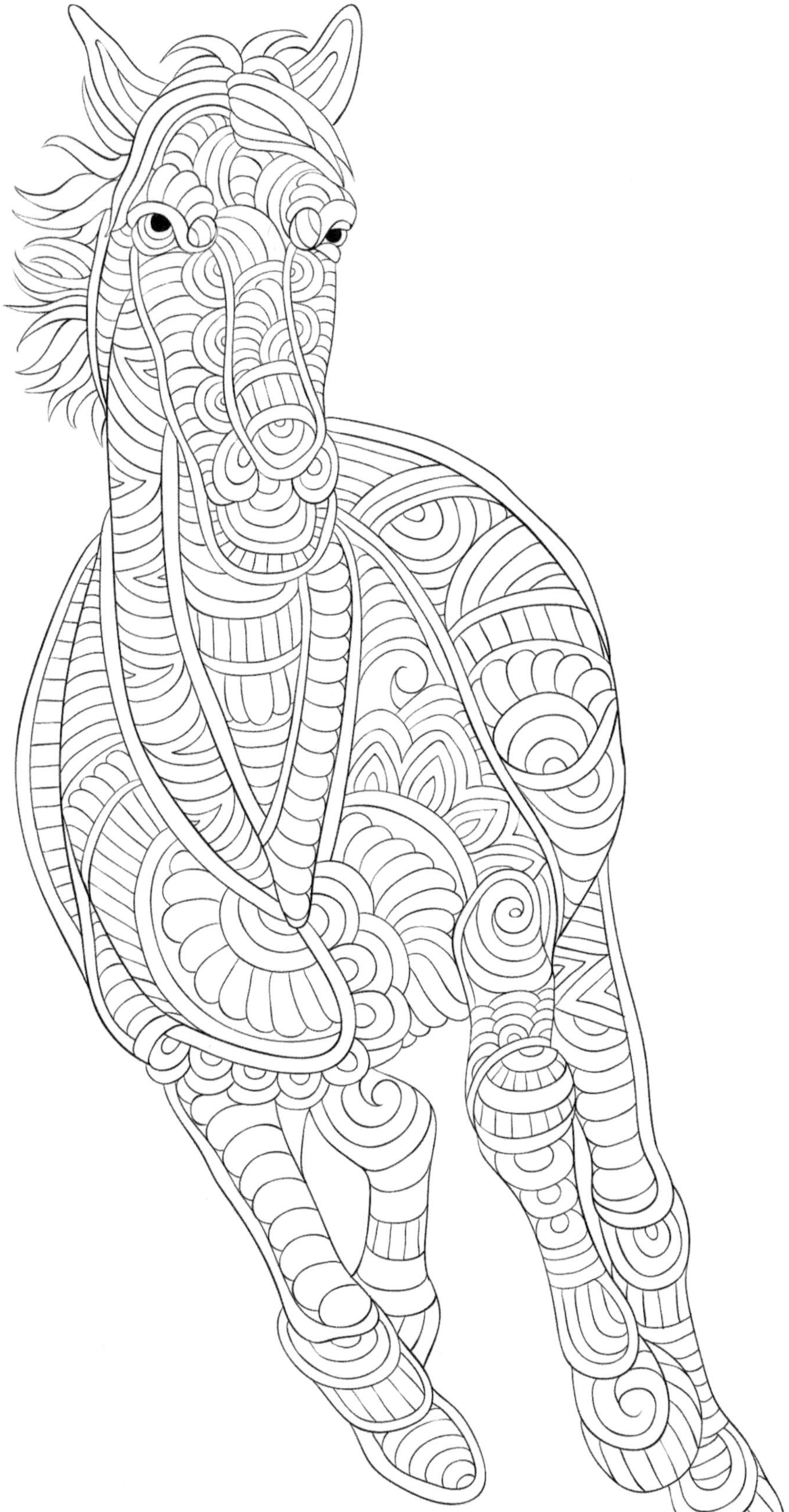

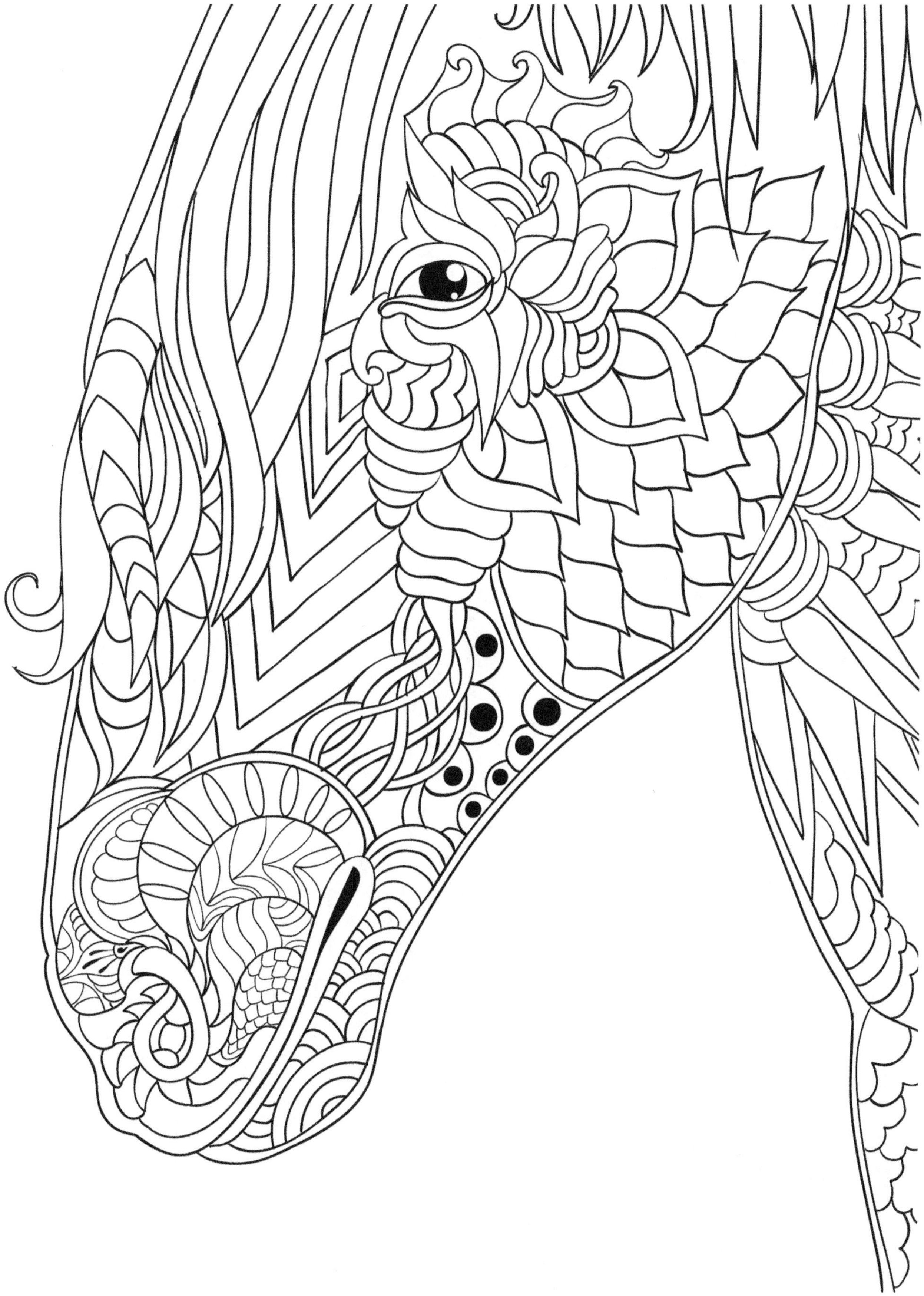

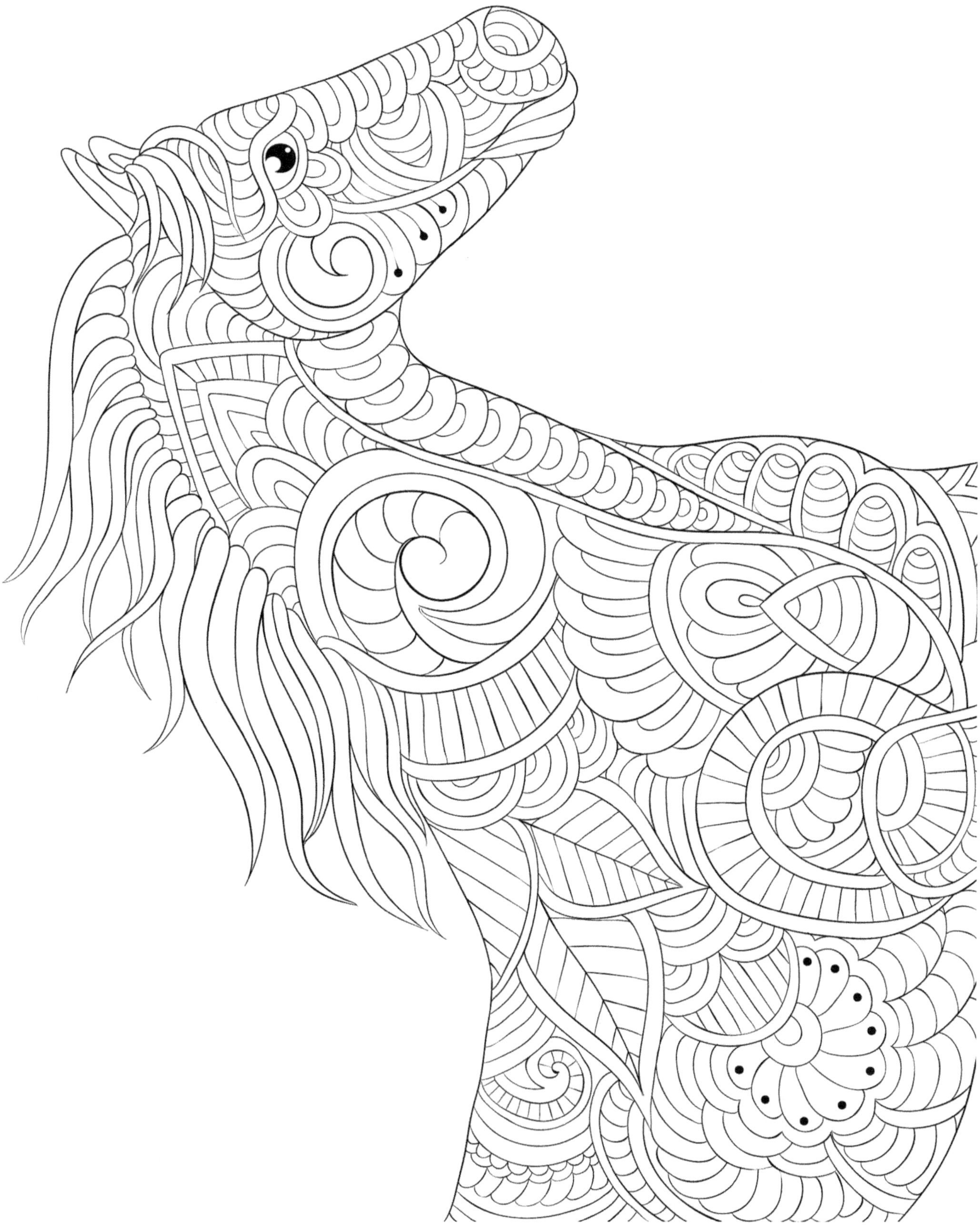

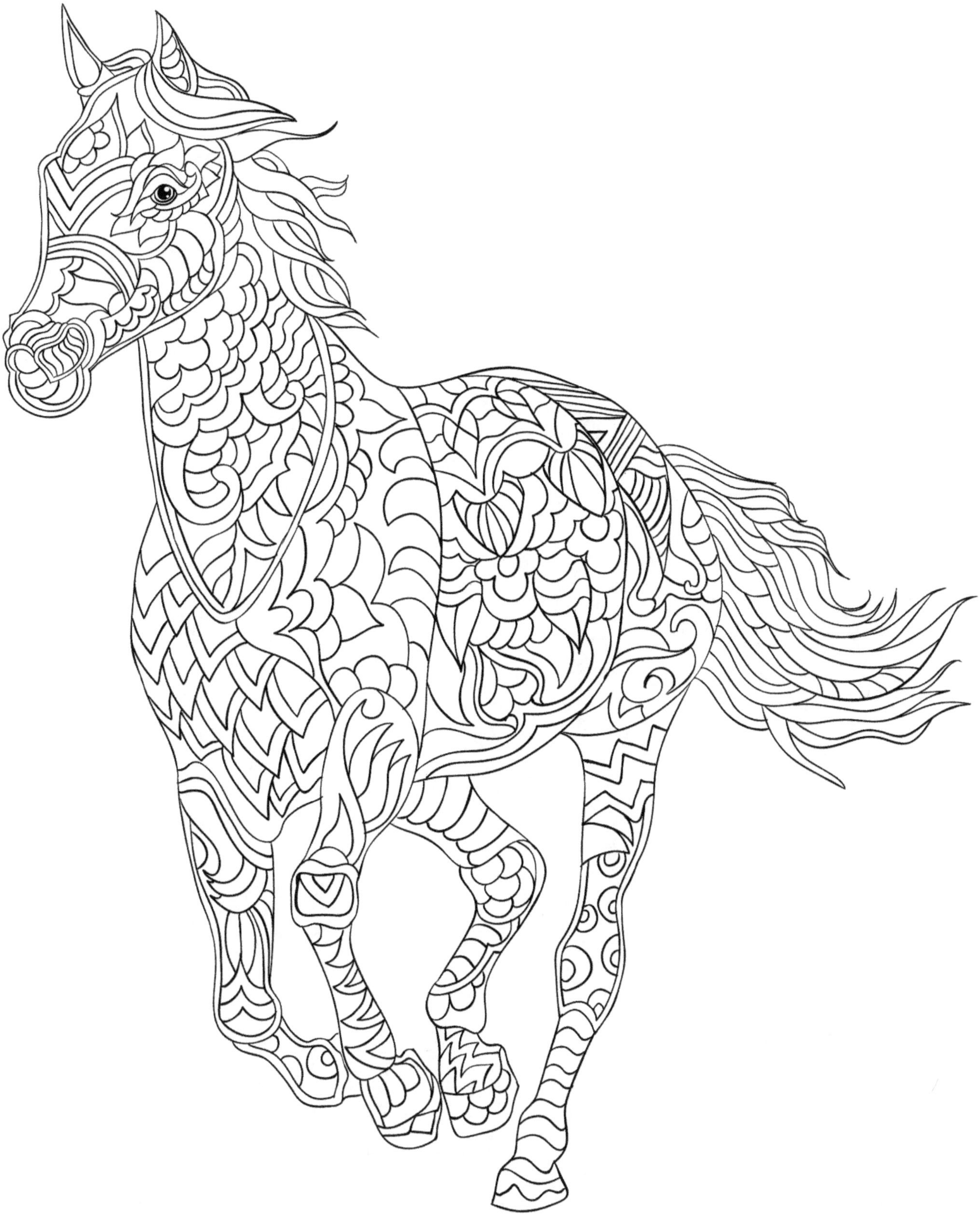

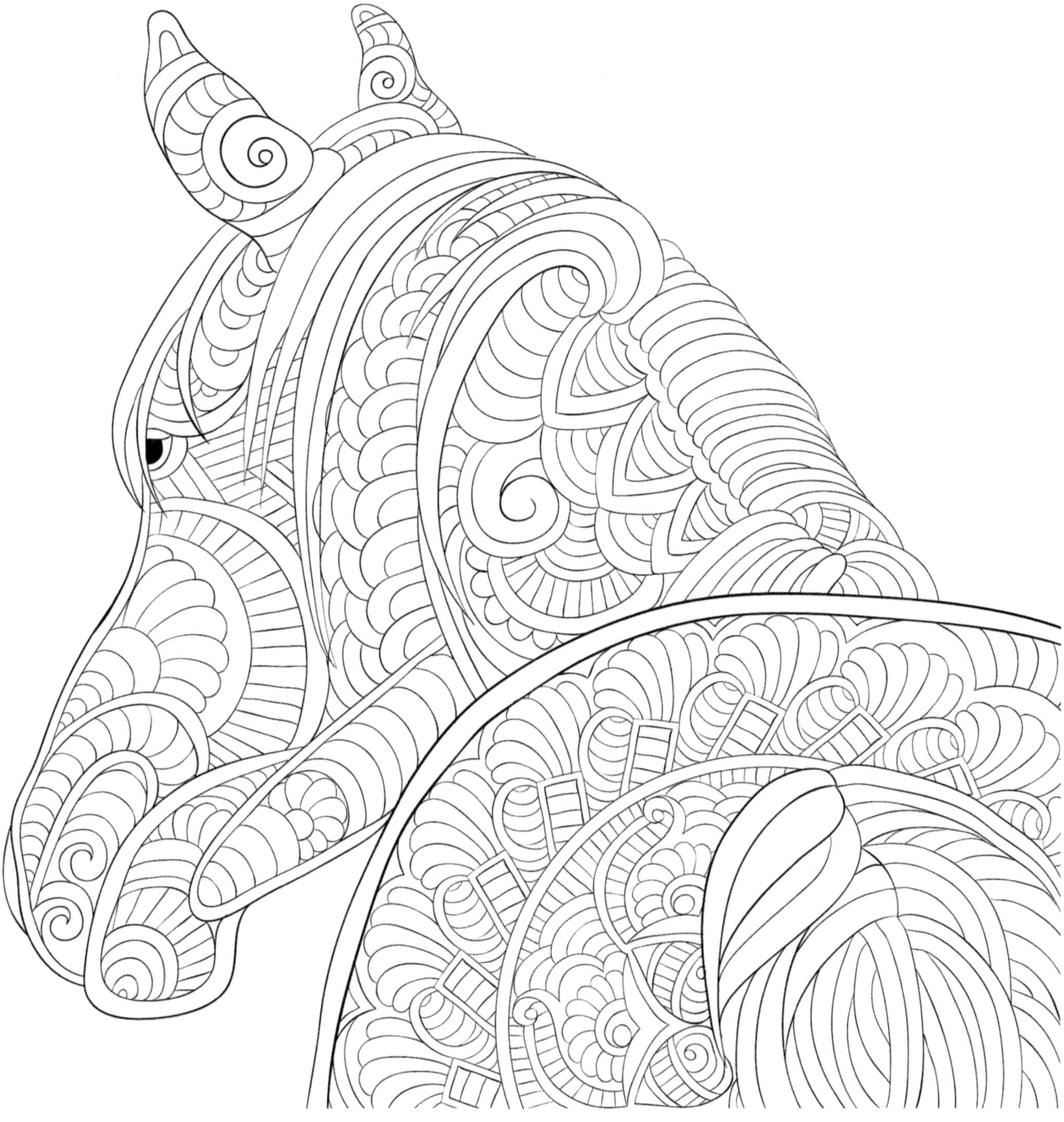

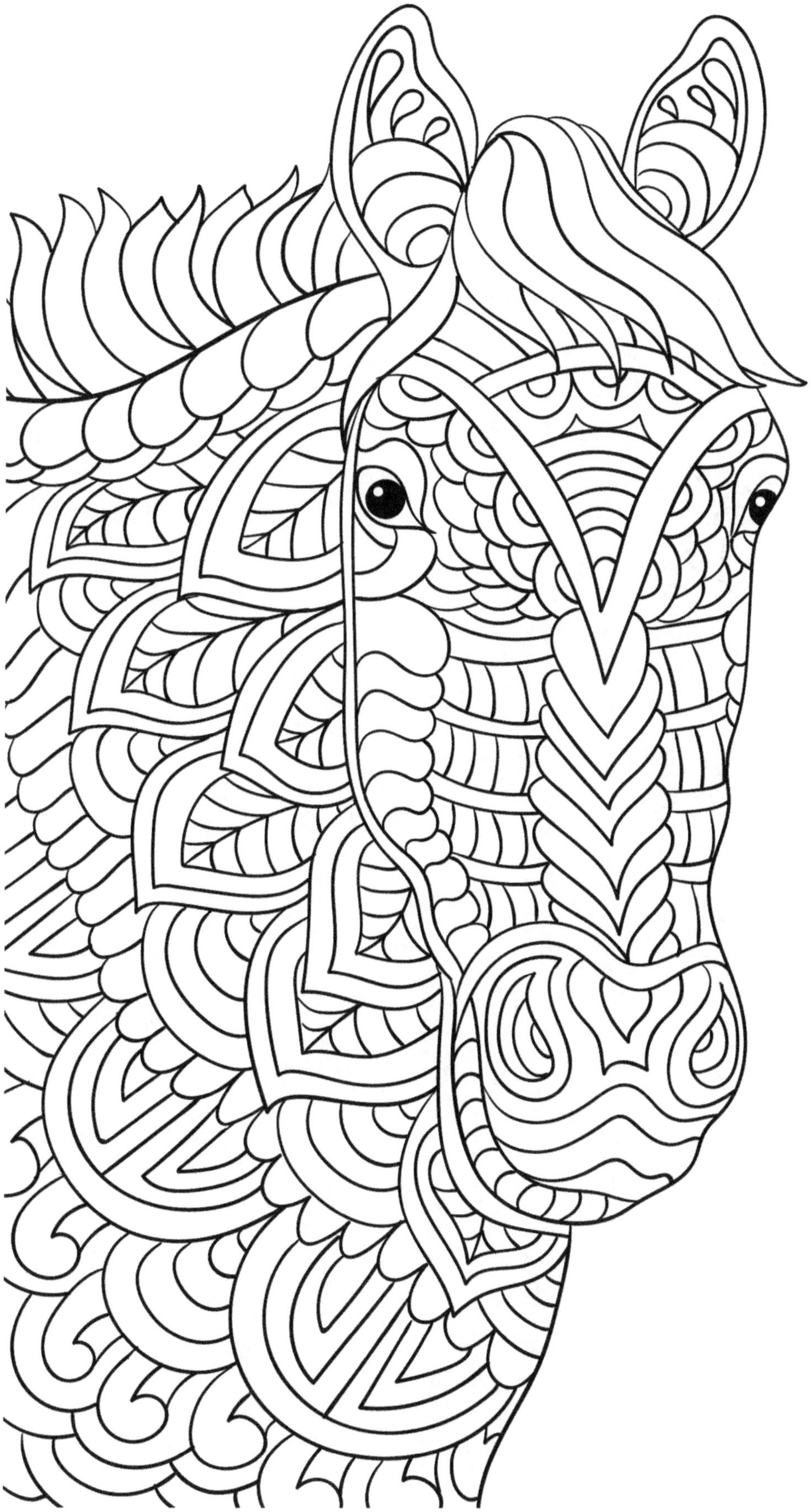

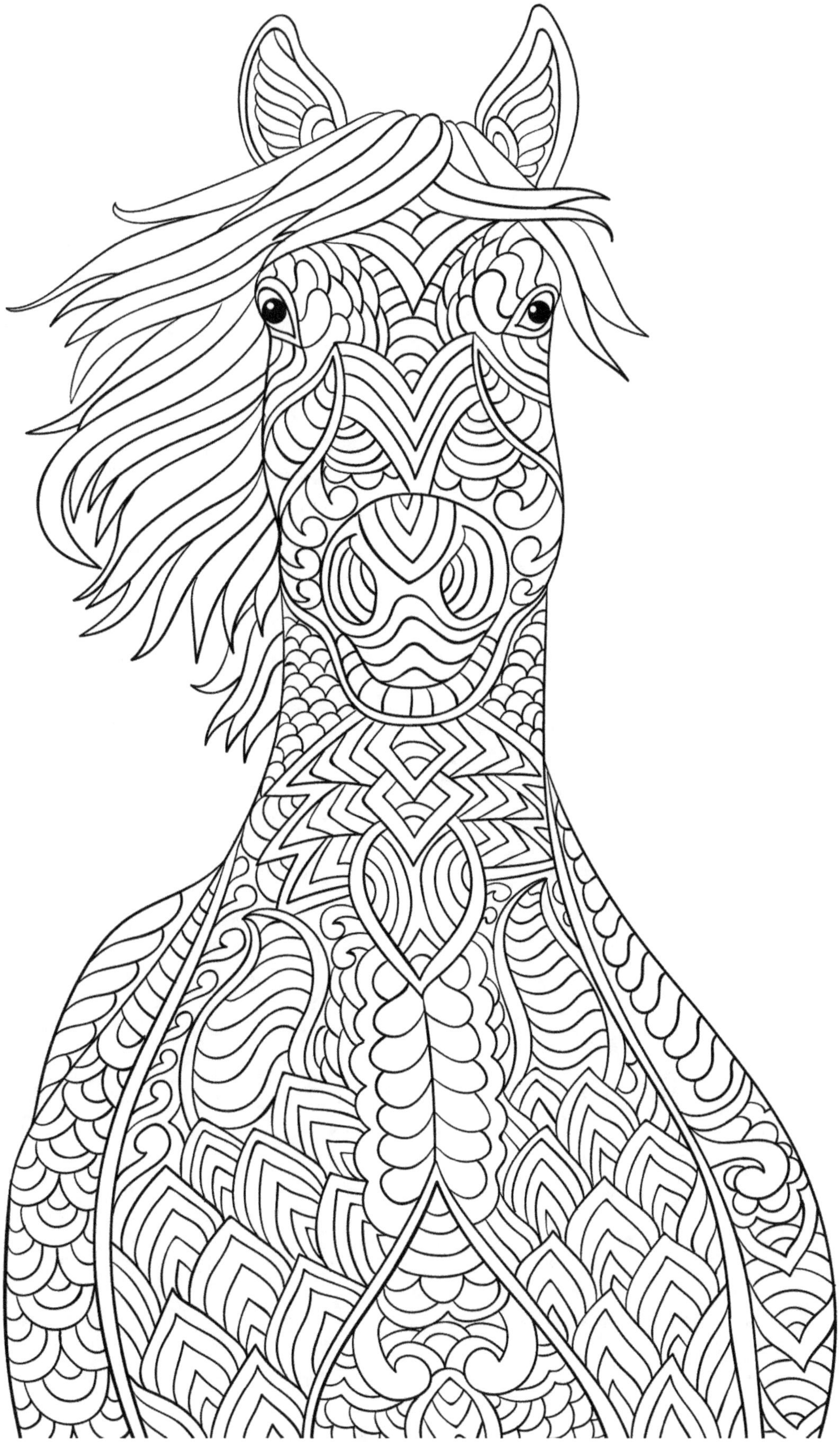

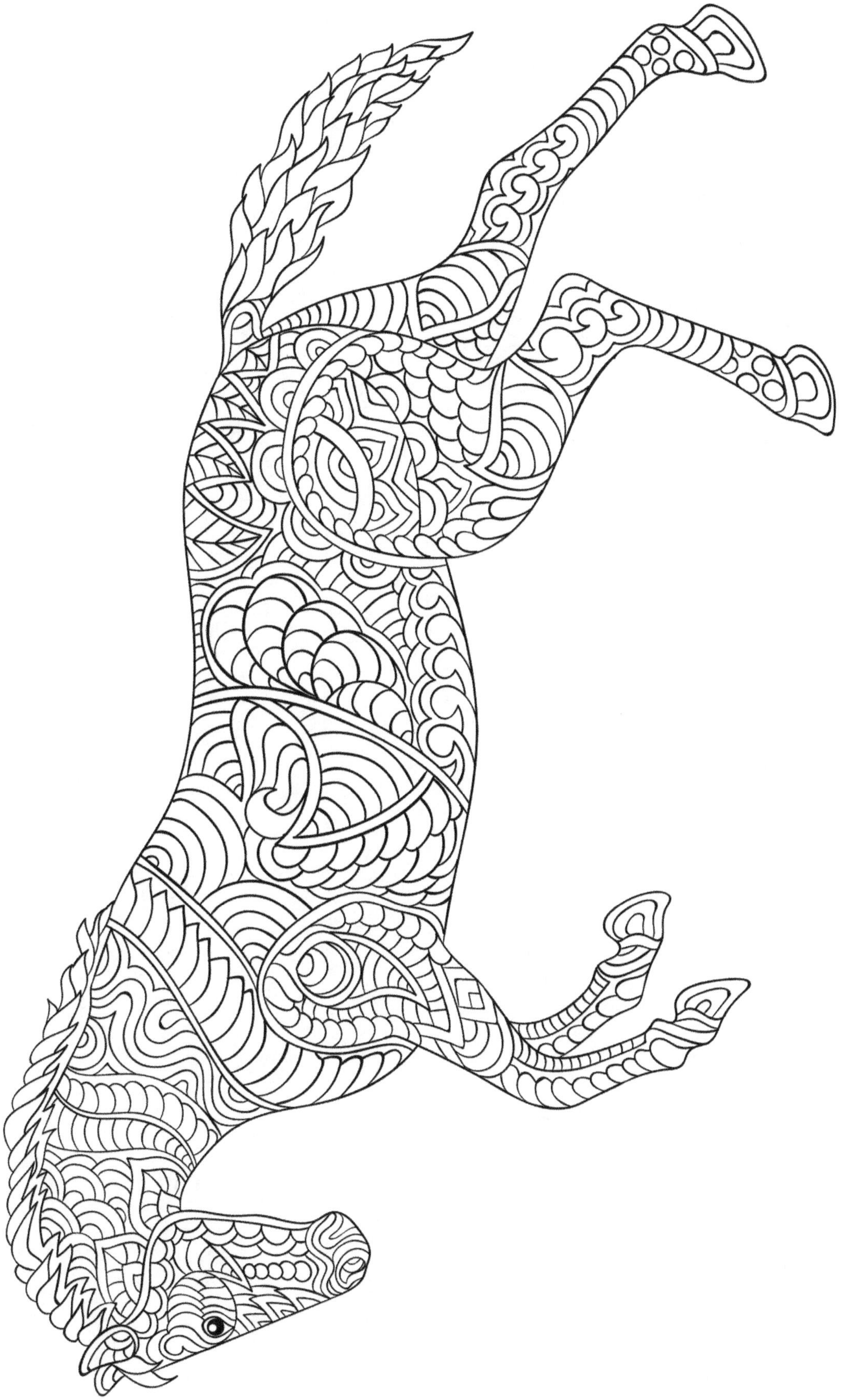

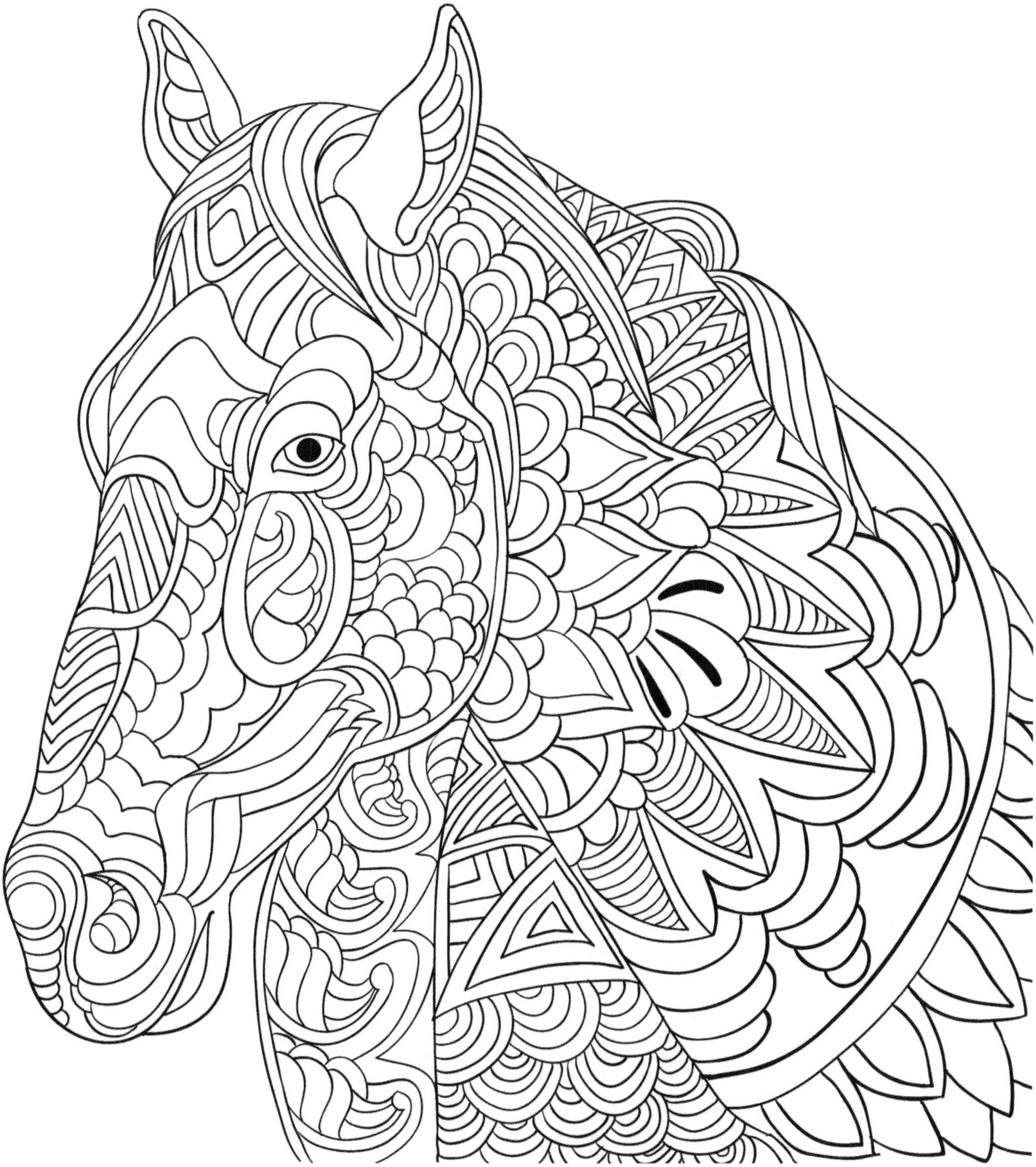

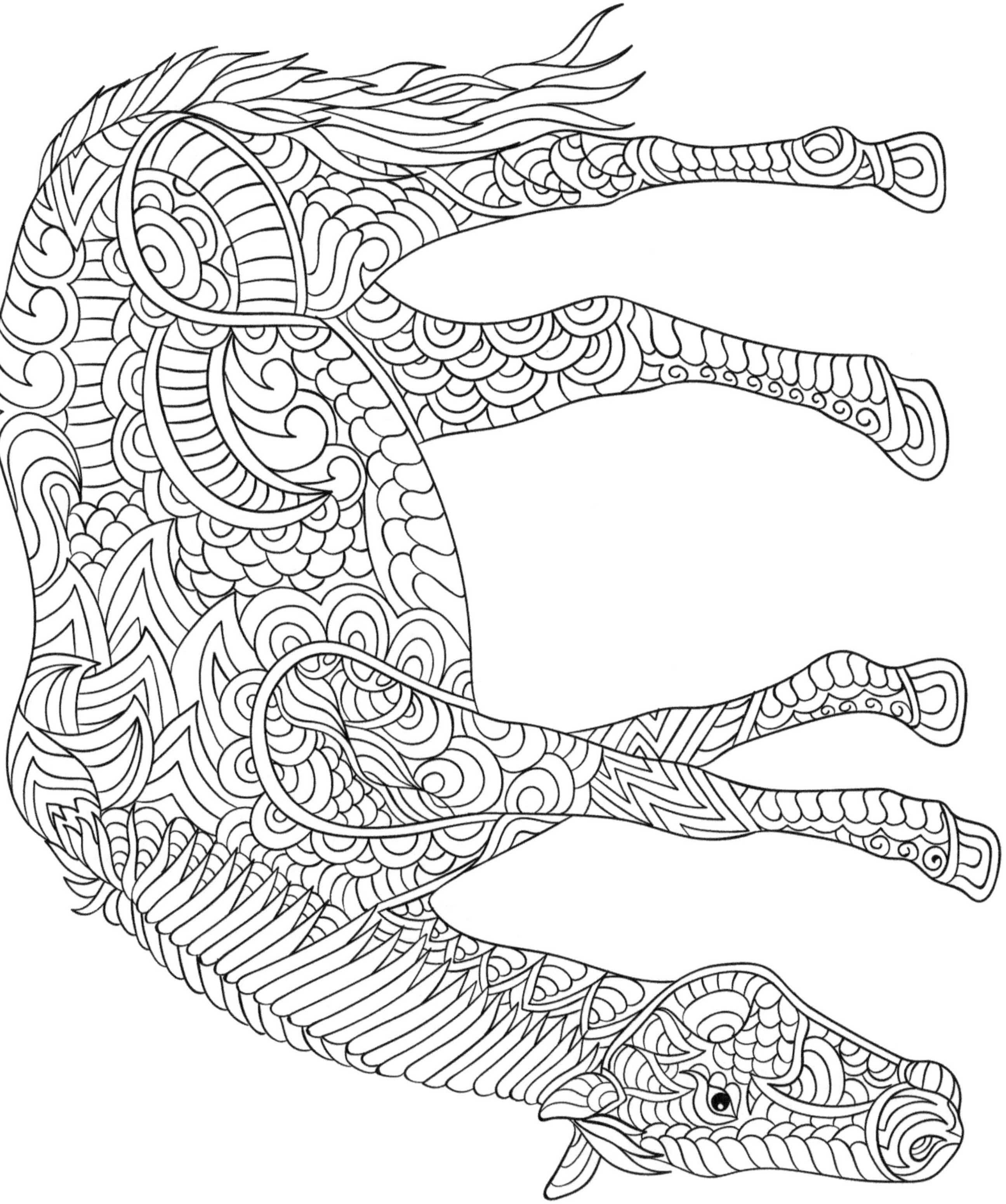

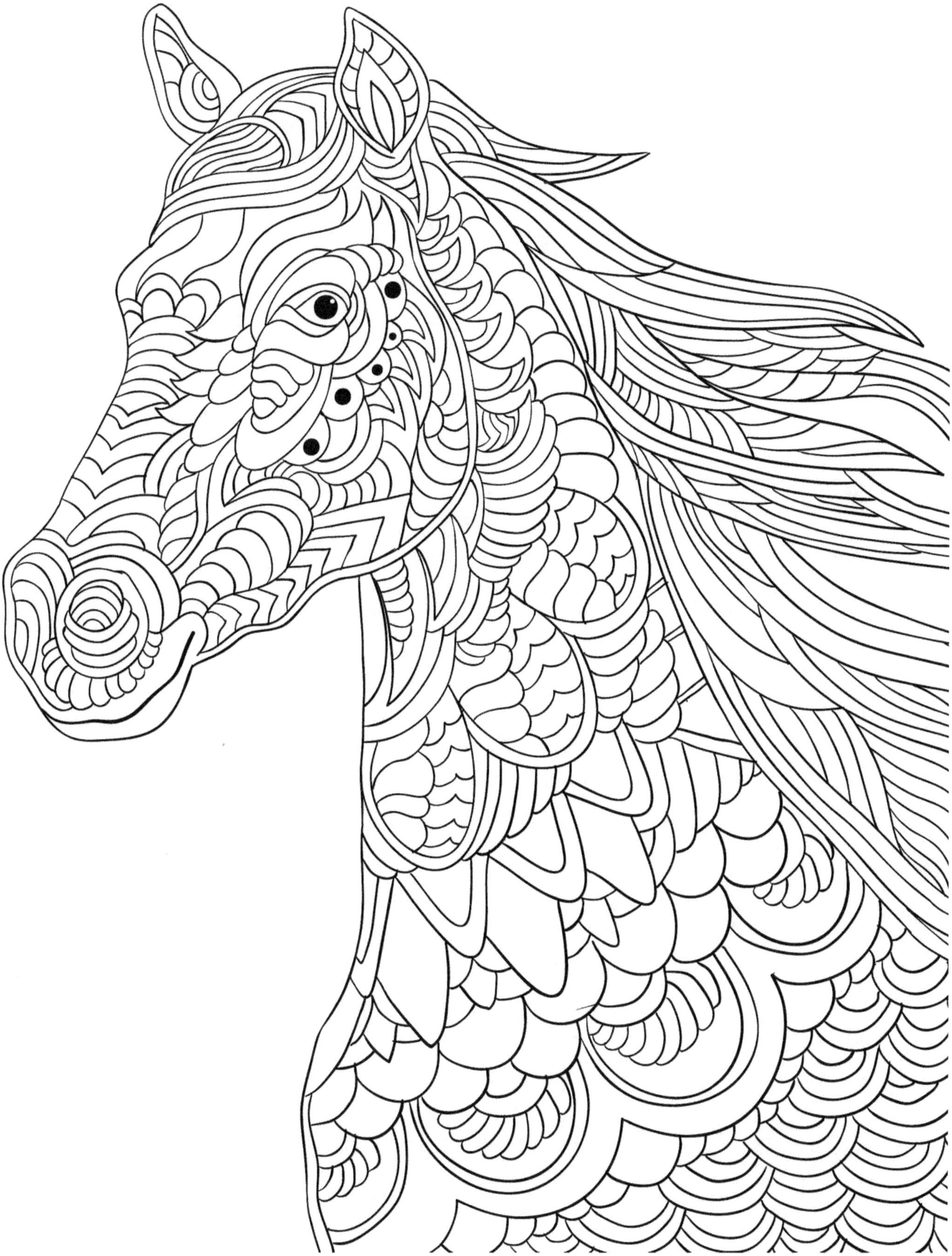

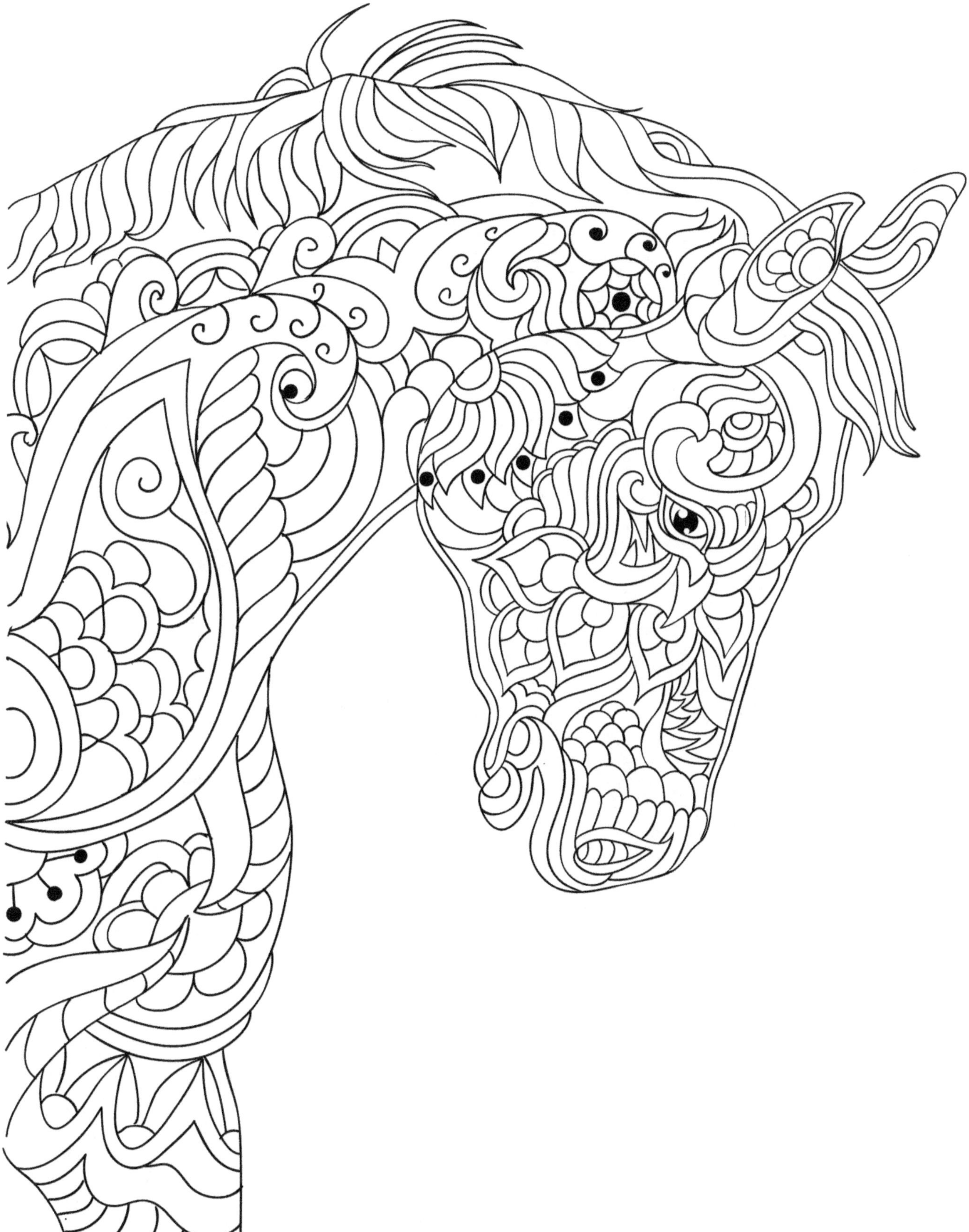

COLOR TEST PAGE

Color Test Page

www.ingramcontent.com/pod-product-compliance
Lightning Source LLC
Chambersburg PA
CBHW080717190526
45169CB00006B/2418
9781533428462